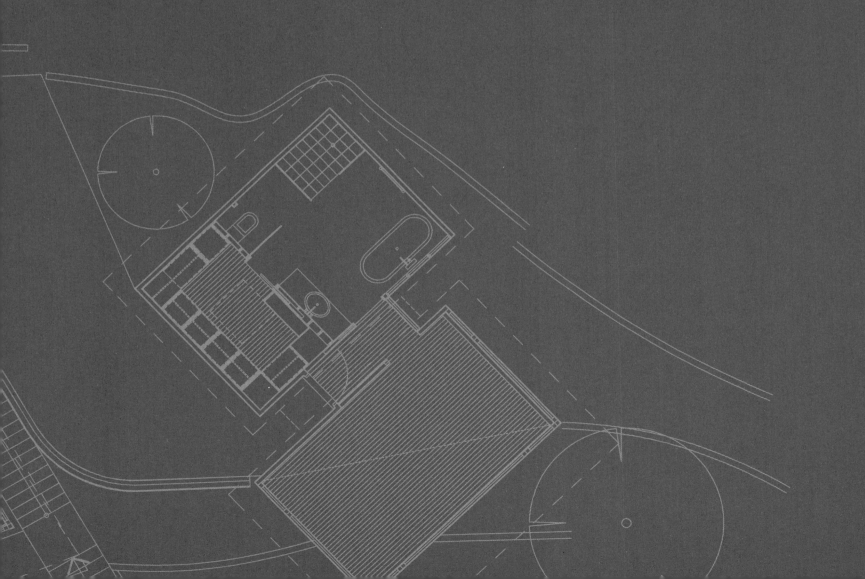

100 Top Houses from Down Under

100 Top Houses from Down Under

images
Publishing

Third reprint 2007
The Images Publishing Group Reference Number: 709

Second reprint 2006
The Images Publishing Group Reference Number: 657

First reprinted in 2005
The Images Publishing Group Reference Number: 652

Published in Australia in 2005 by
The Images Publishing Group Pty Ltd
ABN 89 059 734 431
6 Bastow Place, Mulgrave, Victoria 3170, Australia
Tel: +61 3 9561 5544 Fax: +61 3 9561 4860
books@imagespublishing.com
www.imagespublishing.com

Copyright © The Images Publishing Group Pty Ltd 2005
The Images Publishing Group Reference Number: 626

National Library of Australia
Cataloguing-in-Publication entry:

100 top houses from down under.

Includes index.
ISBN 1 86470 141 2.

1. Architecture, Domestic – Australia – Pictorial works.
2. Architecture, Domestic – New Zealand – Pictorial works.
3. Interior decoration – Australia – Pictorial works.
4. Interior decoration – New Zealand – Pictorial works.

728.0994

Edited by Robyn Beaver

Designed by The Graphic Image Studio Pty Ltd, Mulgrave, Australia
www.tgis.com.au

Film by Mission Productions Limited

Printed by Everbest Printing Co. Ltd, in Hong Kong/China

IMAGES has included on its website a page for special notices in relation to this and its other publications. Please visit www.imagespublishing.com.

The 100 projects featured in the following pages represent some of the finest examples of contemporary residences from Australian and New Zealand architects and designers. The projects include award-winners, luxury residences, simple beach shacks, inner-city apartments, rural retreats and suburban family homes, reflecting the way we live, or aspire to live, in the 21st century. That the projects vary so widely is indicative of the enormous variety and originality in the talent and design direction of architects from 'Down Under'.

Although the projects are diverse in size, location, use, ambience, budget and taste, some common themes are evident. A desire to blend with the surrounding landscape, whether it be a significant heritage streetscape in the inner city, a protected coastal dunescape, or perhaps indigenous bushland, is the aim of many projects. Strikingly contemporary additions and renovations have been thoughtfully inserted behind traditional or heritage façades that give no hint of the often expansive residences they conceal. In rural areas, houses are partially 'inserted' into the earth, so that the building appears as part of the landscape, reducing its visual impact.

The incorporation of sustainable features is another underlying theme that links these residences. Environmental stewardship is important to the architects of Australia and New Zealand and they are keen to exploit the ever-growing range of sustainable features and products. Houses are oriented to achieve cross-ventilation by cooling breezes, often completely obviating the need for mechanical air-conditioning. Natural ventilation is incorporated wherever possible, as are photovoltaic panels and rainwater collection systems. Environmental sensitivity is achieved by the use of natural materials that blend with the landscape, complementing the informal nature of many of these houses. Exposed structural elements add rawness and visual stimulation in keeping with often rugged locations. Simple, durable, easily maintained and versatile materials such as recycled timber, concrete, steel, rammed earth, Colorbond, aluminium and glass predominate, whether to counter the destructive effects of a harsh coastal environment, or to complement a suburban setting.

In terms of structure, a principal theme is the separation of houses into 'pavilions', with each pavilion being assigned a specific use. Often, the house is a collection of discrete buildings, with links providing access from one building to another. Notions of privacy for adults, the separation of living, eating and sleeping zones, specially designed areas for children, or for contemplation or recreation, are important factors in the design of contemporary houses. The separation between private and public spaces is often defined and identified by the use of specific materials and finishes, both internally and externally.

The indoor/outdoor room is another influential feature. The 'Down Under' climate, while extending from tropical to alpine, is well-suited to outdoor living, and the design of contemporary houses reflects and facilitates the outdoor lifestyle. Interiors spill out seamlessly onto outdoor living areas through sliding or folding glazed doors or entire pivoting walls, extending interiors by blurring the distinction between indoors and out. The internal courtyard brings the outdoors in, despite the weather. The continuity of building materials and finishes adds to the 'seamless' nature of indoor/outdoor rooms.

Water is integral to the outdoor lifestyle, whether embodied in the soothing trickling of a sculptural water feature, or the joyous cacophony of children at play in an infinity-edge swimming pool. The Asian aesthetic is also a major influence, whether overt, in the use of Japanese screens or the incorporation of tatami rooms, or more subtly in the simplicity, lack of clutter, and emphasis on tranquillity that is evident in many of these projects.

As expected with a collection of 'Down Under' homes, the locations are spectacular, as are the designers' responses to some challenging environments. Interior windows are placed to capture and frame ocean views; seemingly impossible obstacles are overcome to perch a house high on an inaccessible clifftop; some houses are accessible only by boat, increasing the anticipation and high theatre of the occasion.

The shared characteristics and themes identified throughout this collection of houses might group them into a loosely defined 'Down Under' aesthetic, but each house stands alone as testament to the skills of an individual designer. As you flip through the following pages, you will agree that the architects of Australia and New Zealand have much to be proud of. This book has been a delight to compile, and we hope to follow it soon with a further collection of stunning houses from 'Down Under'.

Robyn Beaver, Editor
The Images Publishing Group

CONTENTS

1A LIVINGSTONE PARADE

ODR

This project is a small house on a small site. The architects' hope was to achieve a building with architectural presence that creates a discourse within a contextual condition. • It is referential in acknowledgment through association, rather than form. Reinterpretation rather than duplication. The adjacent old hospital is a large building made of many small bricks; its giant chimney dominates the urban landscape. The new house is a small building wrapped in giant bricks (pattern on screen); the chimney is celebrated and referenced through an over-exposed flue. The new black corrugated box replaces an existing corrugated shed; memories of the shed are embraced through materiality. The architects 'like to clad an Australian building in black'. • The black box, the giant aluminium brick screen and the over-exaggerated flue are the primary outward architectural gestures. The story is written into the wall. • The informal architectural proposition is; how do you make something small feel like something big? • There is no 'articulation' to reduce visual bulk, rather, the building is 6.5 metres high and abuts a corner without respite. The front door is accessed via the backyard, and the entry is through a 6-metre atrium, something unexpected. On entry, the sky and the internalised deck are visible. Simultaneously, the atrium forms part of the living area in attempting to 'make the space feel bigger'. These void spaces without programme become critical. • Inherent is a proposition of privacy, challenging common perceptions and comforts. During the day the occupants see out, at night others see in. Translucency softens the impact. The screen disguises the programme behind and acts as the mediator. The outside is accessing the inside and programmatic boundaries are continuously called into question. • It makes no apologies for being heroic. Seldom do passersby think it's a home.

2

1   East elevation, showing the referenced brick pattern and chimney

2   House in its suburban context, exposing its references to the old hospital and chimney stacks beyond

3   Ground floor plan

4   First floor plan

1	Deck
2	Living
3	Dining
4	Kitchen
5	Laundry
6	Study
7	Carport
8	Bathroom
9	Bedroom
10	Deck
11	Atrium

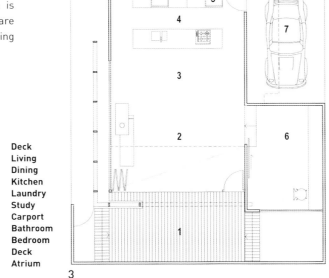

3

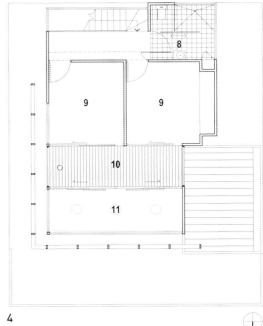

4

5

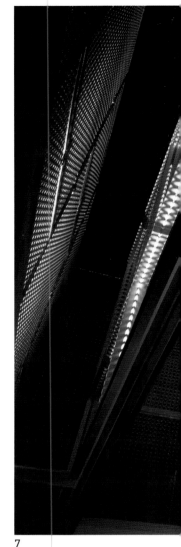

7

6

8

5   Living in one space
6   The private court showing the relationship to the street (behind the screen) and the atrium
7   Entry atrium and private court at night
8   The interior is revealed to the street at night
9   Operable sliding toilet and shower screen

Photography: Derek Swalwell

A I R E Y S   H O U S E

L E O N   L O P A T A

This house is on one of Australia's best-known coastal routes, **Victoria's Great Ocean Road**. The designer's intention was to create a practical and easily maintained beach house, a place for relaxation, family, friendship and freedom. • The design achieves a sense of airiness and space. The raking roof/ceiling line with high windows on both the north and south sides opens up to the sky. The communal spaces are interconnected and designed to allow people to come together and relax while the bedrooms, on the north side of the building, are warm and intimate. A multipurpose room on the lower level opens out to a northern deck that is partially enclosed by a sandstone retaining wall and a timber pergola. • Floor-to-ceiling glass windows frame the sky and coastline, inviting in the drama of the incoming weather. High opening windows allow hot air to flow up and escape, while other lower sliding openings assist in flushing the house with cool breezes, obviating the need for mechanical cooling. • Outside, the 'butterfly' roof naturally forms a large box gutter that collects rainwater, which falls down a steel chain into a water tank on one side of the building. The west wall is built like a shear parapet, designed to protect the building from the hot afternoon sun. At the base of the wall is the timber water tank enclosure, which like a timber block rammed into the earth visually anchors the building. • Materials reflect the surrounding environment. The main structural material is concrete block work, in charcoal, alabaster, and sandstone colours, in two different textures and block laying methods. Glass is used extensively, teamed with black powdercoat-finish aluminium frames; spotted gum is used as a cladding. The exterior also features the use of steel outriggers that support and form the eaves and expressed steel structural members in special marine-quality paint finishes.

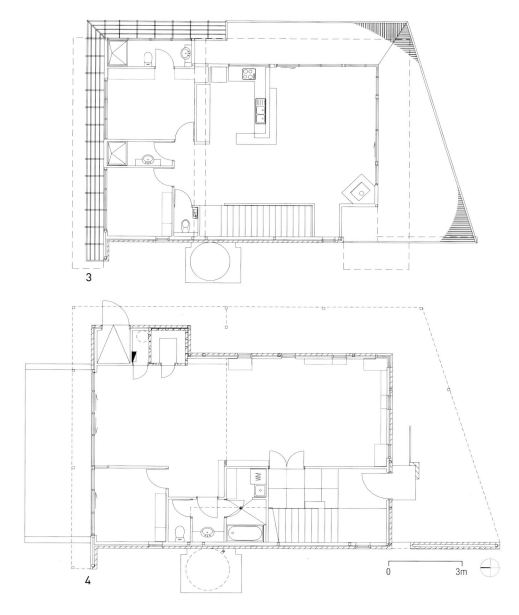

3

4

0   3m

2

Opposite:
   Southeast elevation: high concrete blockwork wall protects as well as anchors the building
2   East elevation with winged roofline
3   First floor plan
4   Ground floor plan

5

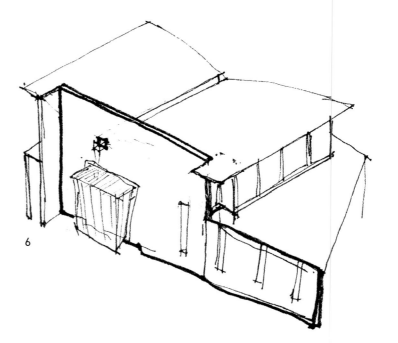

6

7

8

9

5   Combined kitchen, dining and living areas
6   Architect's concept sketch
7   Front decking forms large outdoor space and provides canopy for carport below
8   Kitchen with cherry wood built-in joinery
9   Kitchen with granite bench top and servery with cherry wood cabinets below

Photography: Mark Munro

1

2

ANGLESEA HOUSE

EMMA MITCHELL ARCHITECTS

The project, in **Anglesea** on **Victoria's Surf Coast**, called for the renovation of a two-storey cedar weatherboard house, with the aim of transforming it from a basic 1980's holiday home to a fully functional contemporary permanent residence. While the original home was designed primarily to take predictable advantage of the ocean view, its mediated descendant has been designed to pay tangible respect to the past life of the dwelling, to meld the building more authentically into its natural environment and to create new layers of space which give multiple experiences of the ocean and bush views. • This project has been a significant investigation into what a house embodies and ways in which the house can evolve to meet new requirements as family structures change over time. The idea of memory was a significant point of investigation for the project, retaining spaces, recycling and revivifying materials of significance. • The idea of view, and the issue of how space could be framed and moved through to create varied experiences of a single view, were driving forces for the arrangement of interior and exterior spaces. Asian landscape design and Chinese landscape painting were sources of inspiration for tackling this concept. • The form of the building is an investigation into what defines a beach house type. The form recalls American modernism or that of an ocean liner; the materials used recall old-style holiday homes. The house is an expression of form that is specific to its surrounding environment and specific to the spatial requirements of the brief. Colours and landscaping were chosen to reflect the bush and coast unique to this site.

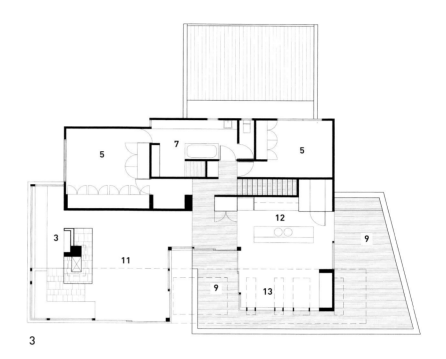

3

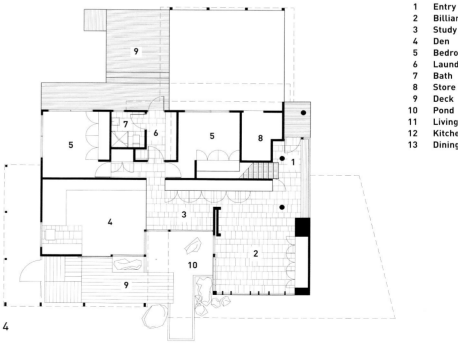

4

1	Entry
2	Billiards
3	Study
4	Den
5	Bedroom
6	Laundry
7	Bath
8	Store
9	Deck
10	Pond
11	Living
12	Kitchen
13	Dining

1   Eastern elevation from street
2   Pond, seen from the den
3   First floor plan
4   Ground floor plan

5   Looking south from the north deck
6   Rasmus the golden retriever enjoying the living room window seat
7   Living room fireplace
8   Kitchen and dining room from the central deck
9   Upstairs bathroom viewed from bedroom door

Photography: Dianna Snape

5

6

7

8

9

1

2

3

4

A P A R T M E N T   4 4

D A V I D   H I C K S   P T Y   L T D

This apartment is located in a prestigious **Melbourne** landmark building, close to the CBD. The north-facing apartment allows views across the Royal Botanic Gardens, and along Melbourne's premier boulevard to the city. • A complete refurbishment of the existing apartment was required to breathe fresh life and elegance into the space. The existing grey granite, beige paint and blue carpet were not complementary to the exterior scenery or the penetrating northern light. The main aim of the design was to bring a sense of light from the outside into the space, while creating a moody and glamorous atmosphere in keeping with a city apartment. • Polished black terrazzo was chosen for the floor, providing clean lines and an alternative to carpet. The black full-gloss reflects the light without creating glare, while the grey chips hide dust and dirt particles. White-painted walls provide a neutral backdrop for the clients' ever-changing and extensive artwork collection. Skirtings and trims were removed from the walls to eliminate excess clutter. Silver corded goat-hair carpet is confined to the two bedrooms, providing a contrast in texture and some underfoot comfort. Cream silk curtains add a touch of luxury to the bedrooms. • The bathrooms incorporate shimmering, oyster-like materials, providing a tranquil environment in which to preen. Moonlight Calacutta marble slab was used on the bench tops and bath surround, with silver-grey mosaic tiles lining the walls. Large panels of silver mirror extend the spaces and glitter with the reflection of the overhead task lighting. All detailing, including fittings and fixtures was kept to a minimum to avoid fuss. Square underslung china basins disappear beneath the marble bench top while all cupboard door handles have been eliminated. • The resulting atmosphere is one of pure elegance and refinement, interwoven with elements of the clients' personalities and tastes.

5

1   View of bathroom with Calacutta marble bathtub and shimmering stainless
     steel cabinet
2   View across living and dining area to kitchen
3   View across kitchen benchtop to Royal Botanic Gardens beyond
4   Sleek kitchen bench in seamless white and shimmering stainless steel
     reflected in mirrored wall
5   Custom-designed stainless steel powder room vanity with moulded sink
6   Eclectic mix of furniture pieces and artwork
Photography: Trevor Mein

6

1

2

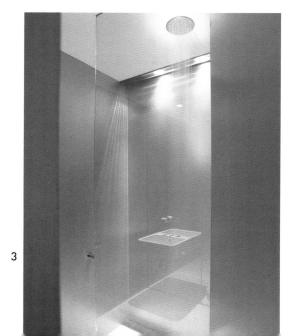

3

4

APARTMENT 302

DAVID HICKS PTY LTD

This apartment is on the third level of a former chocolate factory in **Prahran**, a progressive suburb close to the city of **Melbourne**. The two main features of the building were its high ceilings and open-plan space. • The 100-square-metre, L-shaped footprint presented a number of challenges. With only one south-facing glazed façade, creating a sense of light and space was paramount. By considering scale, reflectivity in materials, and looking to find new ways of construction, the space was transformed into an environment that evokes a sense of extended space. • Given the 3.2-metre slab-to-slab height, a raised platform was incorporated to allow flexibility with the placement of services while allowing the existing concrete slab ceiling to be maintained. A linear bulkhead houses services and provides a strong visual link between the dining and lounge zones. The kitchen was restricted to a 5-metre-long area and all appliances were concealed in a streamlined cantilevered credenza unit. • Attention to detail was very important to the success of the design. A grid formula was conceived, based on the size and layout of the white terrazzo flooring. This allowed the placement of elements such as joinery units to segment the space into zones within the grid. • All materials were detailed to be incorporated as large panels. This over-scaling is evident with the use of silver cladding to seamlessly line the bathroom, and the 6-metre-wide roller blinds made from exterior building screen material. A large mirror panel reflects the entire south façade and maximises the glazing, allowing light to penetrate and further emphasise the suggestion of space. • The combination of the scaling-up of materials, reflectivity, and the choice of seamless products, along with strong planning and utilisation of space, creates an environment that has in fact been minimised to achieve an outcome that has maximised the space.

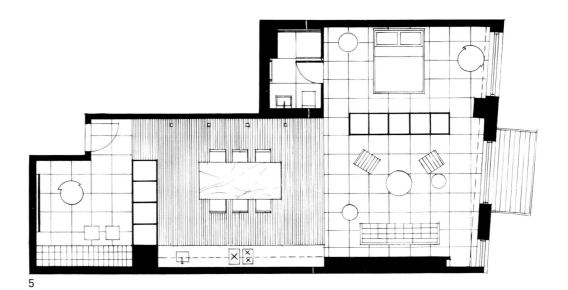

5

1 Living area looking onto raised black gloss timber platform
2 Detail of custom-designed marble and chrome dining table
3 Shower room clad in seamless metallic silver panels; exhaust, lighting and waste all concealed behind grilles
4 Mirrored wall in bathroom conceals storage
5 Floor plan
6 View from living area into bedroom separated by joinery unit which sits on floor tile grid

Photography: Trevor Mein

6

1 Street elevation becomes an external frame for artwork at night
2 Artwork provides a theatrical backdrop to open-plan living spaces
3 Ground floor plan
4 Extensive windows give the sense that courtyards are extensions of internal space

1

2

ART COLLECTOR'S RESIDENCE

CARABOTT HOLT (CH) ARCHITECTS

The narrow **Melbourne** city fringe site influenced the linear planning of this art collector's house, which comprises three bedrooms, formal and informal living spaces and a double-car basement garage. • The house is divided into two zones: an entertaining and living zone and a private zone where the bedrooms are located around two water-themed courtyards that create a bridge-style threshold to the master bedroom. The zoning is achieved with subtle techniques such as raised floors to the formal living area and the use of discrete cavity sliding partitions that disappear from view when open. • The front elevation of the house involves the interplay of cubic volumes with bold red and black accents that are suggestive references to the De Stijl movement of the 1920s. At night this elevation becomes a frame for the centrepiece of the collection, Nolan's *Ned Kelly*, which has a prominent position on the rear wall of the formal living room. This artwork provides a theatrical backdrop when viewed through the expansive glass window from the street outside. • Elements such as the floating black plane that separates the living room from the study serve to challenge perceptions and add to the fluidity of space. The affectionately named free-form 'womb room', prominently accented in bold red is the pivotal element in an otherwise restrained monotone palette of colours and materials. • Natural light is maximised through the design and orientation of the house, its courtyards and windows. The main courtyard is located on the north side of the site to facilitate sunlight into this space and the informal living area. Extensive glazing creates the impression that this courtyard is an extension of the interior of the house. • The design provides an architectural canvas for exhibiting the owner's art collection while creating a series of comfortable living spaces with a simple, stylised décor. The result is a successful integration of architecture and art.

4

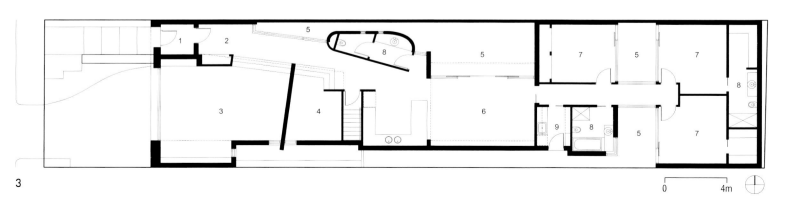

3

1	Porch
2	Entrance
3	Formal living
4	Study
5	Courtyard
6	Informal living
7	Bedroom
8	Bathroom
9	Laundry

0   4m

5

6

5   Water-themed courtyards create a bridge transition to the main bedroom
6   Varied ceiling heights and stepped floor levels provide subtle spatial delineation
7   Doors slide away to invite internal spaces to spill out into external courtyards
8   Interior décor is largely a neutral palette of black and white tones
9   The arrangement of internal spaces creates planned vistas that invite anticipation and curiosity

Photography: Rhiannon Slatter Photographer

7

8

9

1

2

3

ARTHURS SEAT HOUSE

NICHOLAS GIOIA ARCHITECTS

The brief was for a new holiday house on an extremely steep and difficult, naturally vegetated site on Arthurs Seat, on **Victoria's Mornington Peninsula**. The requirement was for a house that was practical, comfortable and affordable, with optimum views of Port Phillip Bay and the coastline. • The architect's response was to design a house that, despite being compact, still feels spacious, admits ample controllable sunlight, and has stunning views. Every habitable room, except for one, is north-facing and has a view of the sea. The north-facing wall of glass has a deep 'picture frame' surround so that the glass is in shadow for most of the summer, but is exposed to sunlight in winter. • The two-storey house includes three bedrooms, two separate living areas, two bathrooms, a dining area, a kitchen and a laundry, within a floor area of 130 square metres. The modest footprint of 68 square metres meant that more than 90 percent of the natural vegetation on the site was left undisturbed. Plywood cladding and other muted, non-reflective external materials allow the building to merge into the environmentally sensitive hillside. • The architectural language is distinctly 'holiday house', and results in a welcoming and restful haven, away from the language of the city house. The house is an exercise in restraint, precision, simplicity and elegance.

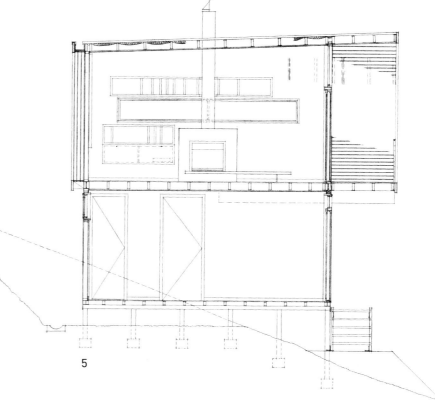

5

4

1   House nestled in landscape (north side)
2   House nestled into hillside (west side)
3   South side of house with bridge from street
4   Ground floor recreation room with master bedroom visible beyond
5   Section

6

7

6   First floor level is a single, pure space
7   Living room in foreground and kitchen beyond
8   View through building to sea beyond
9   Stairway to ground floor is concealed behind
    a horizontal cupboard
    Photography: Trevor Mein

8

9

AVALON HOUSE

CONNOR + SOLOMON ARCHITECTS

This 340-square-metre residence is located within a valley, inland from **Avalon Beach** on **Sydney's northern beaches**. The irregularly shaped site features access via a tree-lined avenue and a small bridge over a traversing creek, leading to a large swamp mahogany tree within a grassed and lightly bushed area. Other similar sites, set amongst the rainforest, surround it. • The house consists of two wings, east and west, flanking the creek edge. The angled wings cradle the rear yard while the glazed link between them is navigated around an ancient Livingstonia palm. • The silted valley floor required the use of lightweight construction on steel torsion piers, while local high wind loads led to the development of a portal steel frame with traditionally framed infill walls. The cladding is Ecoply (plywood) and it is lined in plasterboard, producing an economical house, despite the selection of high-end appliances and fixtures. • Within the east wing are the main living, dining and kitchen areas. It is entered via broad open recycled hardwood stairs, formally delineated by recessed panels housing the pivoting front door. The two-storey entrance space behind is separated from the living areas by the only masonry element of the house. It sculpturally combines the fireplace, stairs and bridge to the upper level main bedroom. • A small link building separates the two wings. The west wing comprises an enclosed verandah that opens into three bedrooms. The bedrooms, while compact, gain actual and perceived space from the verandah via the use of large double doors. • The pared back planning and simple forms belie the complexity of the environmental control strategy. Each space is located to best suit its function and each element is designed to provide some environmental advantage. The controlled openings are positioned to connect each space to the varied parts of the site.

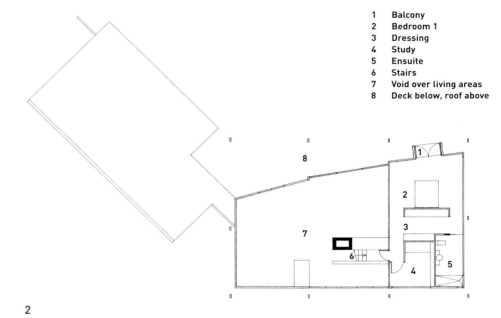

1   Balcony
2   Bedroom 1
3   Dressing
4   Study
5   Ensuite
6   Stairs
7   Void over living areas
8   Deck below, roof above

2

1	Drying area	10	Kitchen/pantry
2	Hall	11	Dining
3	Cellar	12	Verandah
4	Laundry	13	Living
5	Shower room	14	Store/link entry
6	Garage	15	Link
7	Garage entry	16	Bathroom
8	Stairs to upper level	17	Bedroom
9	Entry	18	Verandah room

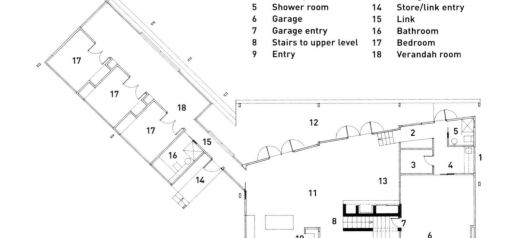

1   North-facing façade with rainforest backdrop
2   Upper level floor plan
3   Lower level floor plan

3

0   5m

4

6

7

5

10

4   View along verandah to children's wing
5   Dining/living looking towards bridge/stairs
6   South elevation and entry
7   Bathroom
8   View along verandah to children's wing at dusk
9   View from dining to kitchen (painting by architect
    Paul Connor)
10 Main bedroom

Photography: Peter Scott

1

2

BIRCH HOUSES

KEVIN HAYES ARCHITECTS PTY LTD

The client's brief was to design two houses that would read as individual dwellings and maintain privacy on a small site in **St Lucia,** a suburb of **Brisbane**. The site offered excellent opportunities. It has good northeastern exposure and lovely neighbourhood views in this direction, while also being sheltered from the west by the natural rise of the land. A mature silky oak tree at the front of the site was a significant feature to be retained. • The spatial organisation of the houses was strongly driven by considerations of how to occupy the site. The massing of the houses is pushed to the southwest corner of the site to maintain access to breezes and views from the northeast. The idea of spaces that 'flow on' softens the rigidity of the fairly strict, efficient circulation spine. This spatial quality is as much defined by the perceptions of the occupant than by distinct enclosure. Space is amplified by the manipulation of light filtering through screens, glazing and rooms and the use of warm, rich materials on a flat, white backdrop reinforces these ideas. Material elements have been assembled in a blunt fashion and structure has been expressed so that the construction technology becomes ornamental.

1   House A, at the front of the site
2   Floor plans, House B (left), House A (right)
3   Exposed, expressive structure was an important aesthetic consideration

3

5

4

4   From the street, the houses read as individual
    dwellings
5   Glazing and screens connect the core of the
    houses to outside
6   Landscape becomes part of the living area
7   Internal spaces are light-filled and open, with
    strong links to outside
8   Internal spaces flow out to external spaces

Photography: Cru Creative

6

7

8

1

2

3

1 Front elevation of both the restored building and sandstone-clad infill
2 Kitchen in infill: stairs to garage on right
3 Rear elevation of infill building: the aluminium-framed doors slide into a pocket seamlessly linking the kitchen to the rear courtyard
4 Upper level floor plan
5 Ground level floor plan

BIRCHGROVE HOUSE

CONNOR + SOLOMON ARCHITECTS

This project is a restoration and reconfiguration of a family home including the addition of a three/four-storey modern infill building. • The original Victorian house, 'Urne', built in the style of a grand terrace, occupied the site next to a sweeping corner once on the route of the **Birchgrove** tramway in **inner-city Sydney**. The 'infill' was built on the previously vacant prominent end site. The infill building acts as a buffer to the busy street and capitalises on spectacular harbour and city views. It matches the original building without competing with it, employing different materials including sandstone within intricate, albeit modern, detailing. • The new building benefits from vertical ventilation (convection) through the roof stair structure, which captures and cross-ventilates the prevailing northeasterly sea breeze. The existing building's roof space was fully insulated and a ventilating clerestory was placed along the hallway. The latter provides additional natural light to the previously gloomy interior spaces. • Positioned on a noisy corner, the new building acoustically and visually isolates the indoor and outdoor living areas of the original building, placing a robe and pantry/kitchen adjacent to the street edge. Now all outdoor and indoor living areas address one another rather than neighbouring buildings and the street. • A significant feature of the new addition is the sliding doors between the new eating area and the courtyard that track into a pocket adjacent to the kitchen bench. When fully concealed, there is a borderless link between the outside and inside spaces. • Exposed structural steel elements bound the various façade components. On the front elevation, steel flat sections flank the sandstone cladding and frame the fenestration. Likewise structural steel sections within the ceiling zones are expressed on the rear elevation. The sandstone cladding to the front elevation was selected to sit happily against the detailed Victorian façade and stone street (once tramway) cutting. It returns part way along the side elevation, emphasising the corner.

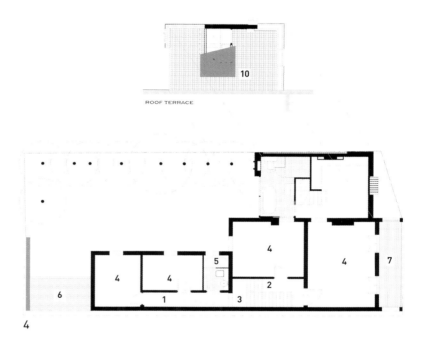

1   Hall with clerestory
2   Refurbished hall
3   Refurbished stairs
4   Refurbished bedroom
5   New boys' bathroom
6   Roof to new laundry
7   Refurbished verandah
8   Infill building with robe and ensuite
9   Stairs to roof terrace
10   Roof terrace

1   Refurbished entry and entry steps
2   Refurbished hall
3   Refurbished stairs
4   Refurbished dining
5   Refurbished living
6   Refurbished family
7   Refurbished studio
8   New laundry
9   Courtyard
10   Ground level deck
11   Infill building with kitchen
12   Pantry
13   Stairs from garage
14   Juliet balcony
15   Infill building with garage
16   Stairs to kitchen

0   5m

6

7

8

9

10

6 Kitchen in infill building
7 Main bedroom: stairs to roof terrace in background
8 Restored dining room looking to kitchen in infill building through refurbished openings
9 Detail of elevational treatment of infill building against restored building with detailed parapet and chimney
10 Infill building against restored building viewed from the rear courtyard

Photography: Steve Garland

1

2

3

BLUESTONE CHURCH CONVERSION

MULTIPLICITY IN ASSOCIATION WITH MEL OGDEN

This former church is in a small town in **regional Victoria**. As architect and designer, Multiplicity, in conjunction with landscape sculptor Mel Ogden, was keen to allay community concern over the fate of the former church and to re-establish and reinterpret the building's role in a small country town. • Architecturally, the built fabric was slowly transformed, as work was split into two stages: harsh weather conditions prolonged preliminary site works to address basic amenity such as the provision of services (electricity, phone, water and a sewerage system). The design called for minimal incursion externally and for the interior architecture to be separate from the original built envelope. • A fairly comprehensive brief was to be accommodated without blocking sightlines within the building from north to south, preserving the two major stained glass windows. Internal spaces designated for private use were expressed as two vertical stacks offset from either side wall with a corridor between. Each stack contains 'pods' on each level; the eastern stack contains bunk bedrooms at both ground and mezzanine levels; the other provides for laundry and shower rooms at ground floor level and provision for a bathroom at mezzanine level. • Part of the living space is deliberately compressed by locating the main bedroom directly above, at almost the full width of the church – cantilevered to not touch surrounding walls and itself only partially enclosed by cabinets. A catwalk links the main bedroom and upper pod levels, cantilevering beyond to provide for a pulpit-like study. • The entry sequence was reversed, with car parking to the rear along an existing carriageway and access to the church itself being redirected either through the small sacristy vestibule or through the 'cloister garden' to the west. The perimeter was fenced in the rural tradition, with hedge planting circumnavigating the property so that over time, the site becomes more private than communal, yet in keeping with the tradition of church architecture.

1   The building sits within a landscape re-worked by Mel Ogden
2   Basalt boulders shown against a sculptural composition of three steel blades within the landscape
3   Cloister garden enclosed with quartzite stone is now the formal entry
4   Former front entry with new steel and glass insertion concrete poem by artist Patrick Jones beneath
5   The purpose-built dining table sits against a backdrop of the two main double-height elements or 'pods', which have bathrooms and children's bunk bedrooms on both levels

4

5

6

7

6   Fireplace supports the mezzanine-level main bedroom, which creates a sense of intimacy and enclosure in an otherwise open-plan living environment

7   Main bedroom at mezzanine level is situated below the principal north-facing window

8   Kitchen design responds to the scale of the former altar

9   The utilitarian downstairs shower room makes the most of available light

10   Newly inserted structural elements are kept separate from original walls and help formalise the arrangement of spaces

11   Acrylic, timber and steel bookshelves frame this edge of the living room

Photography: Emma Cross, Gollings Studios (1,4–11); Alison Pouliot (2,3)

9

8

10

11

1

1   View of kitchen with bedroom 2/study and library beyond
2   View of building in street context
3   Deck with surrounding buildings
4   View of staircase
5   Internal living area
6   First floor plan
7   Ground floor plan

Photography: Peter Fisher

2

3

4

B M G   R E S I D E N C E   /   A R T   G A L L E R Y

TRIDENTE ARCHITECTS

This residence and art gallery establishes an architectural rhythm to a dilapidated streetscape of open carparks, workshops and warehouses in **inner-city Adelaide.** • The design reflects the concept of modern inner-city living, addressing issues of privacy, security and flexibility. • The sharp red box sits proudly within the streetscape with its robust walls built hard against the site boundaries. The façade is articulated by a deck overlooking the gallery's sculpture court, puncturing the façade and cantilevering over the footpath below. • Externally, the gallery, with its uninterrupted boundary walls, directly addresses the social considerations of the site context. Reinforcing the need for security, the only fenestration to the façade is a corner window into the bedroom and a small window to the bathroom. • Internally, the spaces are bathed in sunlight from both the sculpture court at the entrance of the gallery and the slot courtyard to the rear of the gallery. The narrow skylight above the stair to the entrance slices through the residence, washing the sloped wall beneath with natural light. • The complete separation of the residence and the gallery allows the two functions to coexist without overlap. The public space occupies the ground floor, and the residence occupies the first floor; each has a dedicated entrance. • The concept's predominant environmental strategy was to maximise the use of natural ventilation. The ground floor can be completely opened to the outside offering the opportunity for the gallery to operate in an 'outside' sheltered environment. The use of overhangs limits the penetration of direct heat loads into the space. • Budget constraints required the project team to minimise all components of the building. The approach adopted was to utilise the existing structure, wherever possible, maximising the potential of the building footprint.

6

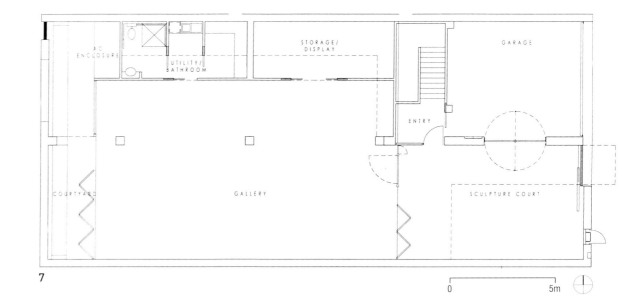

7

0   5m

5

1

2

3

BROADBEACH APARTMENT

POD INTERIOR DESIGN

This project involved the remodelling of a 230-square-metre, northeast-facing apartment with extensive views of the Pacific Ocean near **Surfers Paradise** in **Queensland**. • Existing oak timber floors and white two-pack joinery became the palette base, allowing for an interesting mix of refined and textured elements to feature in contrast. Elements of beach culture were used to create the texture and a natural feel to the spaces. The use of driftwood and sand tones adds warmth within the crispness and freshness of the shell. A custom-designed driftwood sculpture leads the eye from the lounge to the dining area. Textured fabrics contrast against the smoothness of white leather and crisp white bedsheets. • The entry point is directly into the lounge area. A sculptural furniture piece by New Zealand furniture maker David Trubridge features, and reinforces the 'beachy' elegance of the space. Conventional artwork is kept to a minimum, allowing quality pieces to be selected, adding an element of drama and punch to the spaces. • The lounge furniture is multifunctional, allowing coffee tables to be ottomans, side tables to be stools, the lounge to be a bed, catering to the varying numbers of family and guests. The square dining table was positioned to enjoy hinterland sunsets. • The client's main focus, being an avid entertainer and cook, was on the kitchen. A large island bench incorporating storage, cooking and seating became the centrepiece of the space. Minimal changes were otherwise made to 'freshen' the look. An outdoor bar setting was a perfect place for afternoon drinks and children's meals. • All beds were custom-designed to meet individual storage requirements, and budget. The children's bedroom was designed to fit as many sleeping options as possible, incorporating trundle-style bedding and extensive storage.

1   Elements of beach culture
2   Kitchen island bench
3   Lounge and dining
4   Bedroom

Photography: David Sandison

4

1

2

3

4

BUDD'S BEACH RESIDENCE

POD INTERIOR DESIGN

This 210-square-metre house is located at Budd's Beach, close to **Surfers Paradise** on the **Queensland** Pacific coast. The client's many aesthetic and functional requirements for this extensive renovation project were incorporated into the design brief. • Major demolition work was required to the stair, kitchen and bathroom to open up the space and maximise natural light. The balcony was also demolished to make way for a timber deck and generous concrete stairs. The client undertook his own landscaping, with the idea of creating a cooling entry and outlook to the house. Bamboo predominates as do boulders seemingly strewn through the garden. • The client is an avid collector of art and antiques, items that required integration into an otherwise minimalist space. He also entertains regularly and enjoys company while cooking. This led to the design of a central kitchen island bench that houses all appliances, sinks and preparation space. A solid timber cantilevered countertop functions as a dining and gathering zone with custom-designed stools below. This solid timber element also serves to complement and integrate the antique furniture that occupies the space. • An open stair was designed to further the illusion of space. The stair treads are crafted from the signature black wattle timber hand-selected from northern Queensland. A low storage unit sits below, forming a stair tread. A bamboo-coloured wall connects the two levels and forms the balustrade. • Timing was paramount in this project, and it was completed within three months from the initial design to the end of construction.

6

1	Preparation area
2	Entry deck
3	Stair balustrade detail
4	View from stair
5	A gathering place
6	Kitchen detail

Photography: David Sandison

5

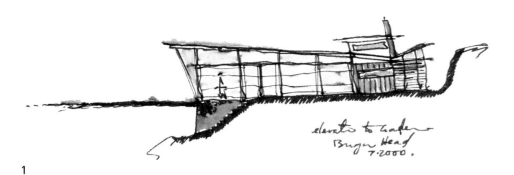

elevate to water
Bryon Head
7.2000.

BUNGAN BEACH HOUSE

DAWSON BROWN ARCHITECTURE

The house is located on a steep southeast-facing slope, high above **Bungan Beach**. It has spectacular views of the beach and flanking rocky headlands as well as the northern beaches coastline to **Sydney**. • The inspiration for the home was the simple, small, monopitched fibro beach shacks of the 1950s and 1960s, translated into today's architecture. • Terraced into the hillside, the building is set on a high random stone base, an extension of the existing massive stone retaining wall adjoining the drive. The stone walls criss-cross the site, stabilising the hill and providing level ground on which to build. • The house is a series of timber pavilions, each with its own function, located around a sun-drenched courtyard. The pavilions sit on or over the stone walls, creating a deliberate dramatic effect of houses perched on a cliff. • The simple monopitch roofs minimise the buildings and open up the interiors to the amazing views. The buildings, with their small-scale layout, dark colours and materials, consciously endeavour to diminish their presence in the landscape. The large overhangs and high stone walls protect the glazed areas from neighbours' views, yet draw in light while shading summer sun. • The buildings are of steel, clad in timber with metal roofs. Floors are of blackbutt timber and walls are lined in hoop pine plywood. The external decks are teak; copper hoods protect windows and doors from driving storm rain.

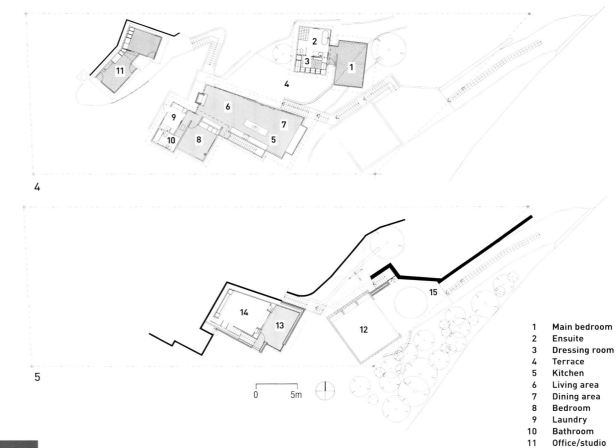

1	**Main bedroom**
2	**Ensuite**
3	**Dressing room**
4	**Terrace**
5	**Kitchen**
6	**Living area**
7	**Dining area**
8	**Bedroom**
9	**Laundry**
10	**Bathroom**
11	**Office/studio**
12	**Garage**
13	**Gym**
14	**Theatre**
15	**Driveway**

1   Architect's sketch
2   Side view of main pavilion
3   Front of main pavilion
4   Upper floor plan
5   Lower floor plan

8

6 Pavilions at dawn
7 Kitchen view
8 Ensuite bath view
9 Section

Photography: Richard Powers

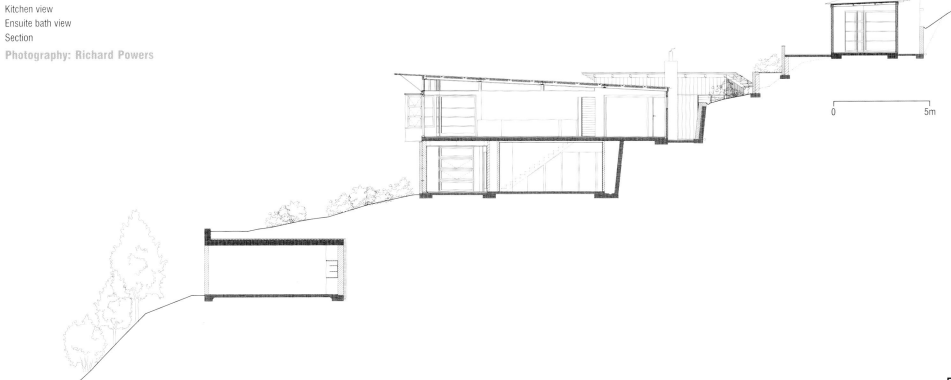

0   5m

9

1

2

1   South façade to shared roof terrace
2   View of Sydney CBD to the west
3   Bedroom joinery
4   Kitchen
5   Main entry/arrival
6   Northern terrace has views to Sydney Harbour
7   Joinery detail

Photography: Murray Fredericks

3

CHALLIS PENTHOUSE

mac-interactive

This residence began as a one-bedroom apartment on the top floor of a 1930's residential block. It was transformed into a two-bedroom penthouse by knocking a hole through the existing roof and building a new 'pavilion' on the existing flat roof. This new pavilion at the north side of the building has uninterrupted views to the west that include **Sydney Harbour** and the city skyline. • The structure is a lightweight steel frame, prefabricated off-site, erected and then dismantled, to speed up construction, minimise site times, crane costs and disturbance to local residents. It is also part of the desire to 'tread lightly' and promote sustainable design. • By presenting a fairly solid elevation to the south and east sides, the new extension protects the privacy of the new owners, the immediate neighbours and other residents using the common area immediately to the south. These two façades to the south and east are clad in a palette of flush-seam copper, recycled timber and opalescent white glass. • The other two façades to the north and west are completely glazed and slide away to open this level up to the wraparound terrace and the views and also provide fantastic opportunities for natural cross-ventilation. In this open configuration the roof acts like a giant shade structure. • The roof is set back from the main volume of the pavilion and is 'lifted up' to emphasise the lightweight nature of the design (through the use of clerestory glazing) and to form a connection to the sky. This also allows any solar heat build up to escape naturally. • This natural ventilation is further assisted by treating the staircase as a chimney, 'roofed' over with a grille to minimise loss of floor space. The grille also coincides with the location of the gas fireplace, which means that in winter the heat is circulated much faster than normal through natural convection currents.

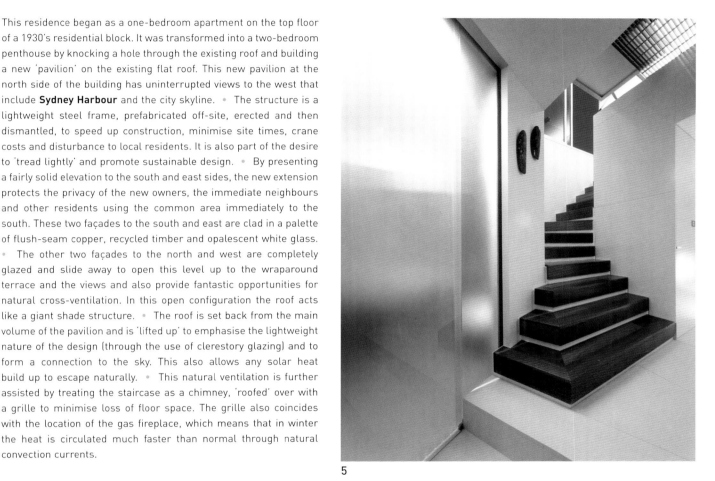

5

6

4

7

1

2

CHAMELEON

CASSANDRA COMPLEX

The site is a turn-of-the-century industrial warehouse in a homogenous strip of six in inner-city **Melbourne**. The building sits hard up against the street, metaphorically interpreting Walter Benjamin's suggestion of culture being most dynamic when the veil is thinnest. There is no threshold here, no front yard. Thus, a secondary internal veil was installed by way of a perforated gold door. The new door suggests the beginning of a reimagined history embedded within the discarded object that previously housed an auto electrical business and before that, a confectionery factory. •
The brief was to design and construct a space that is deliberate and uncertain, to extend private imperatives into a public domain, using architecture as the medium. The ultimate aim was to represent the client's desired autonomy in a spiralling world, while maintaining the physical integrity of the warehouse. • A tour of the house begins with the kitchen, which can be viewed from the main living space, through a slice of the glowing 'ruby'. Continuing the tour, to the right is a storeroom, followed by the second bathroom (a combination of reflecting mirrors) to the left, the bedroom wing and then finally the kitchen. The bedroom occupies the southwest corner, which links through to the main bathroom via a walk-through dressing space with openings. A large rhomboid bath links the bathroom to the living space, dissolving conventional separation; the shower screen is a large lightweight gate. The acute angle of the bedroom is negated by a mirrored wall with a window appearing to float in space. • On the mezzanine level, one is perched up above the 'ruby' within the cosy cinema space and a guest quarter. Continuing up to the roof deck, one finds a hammock, a spa, a barbeque and stunning views across the city of Melbourne.

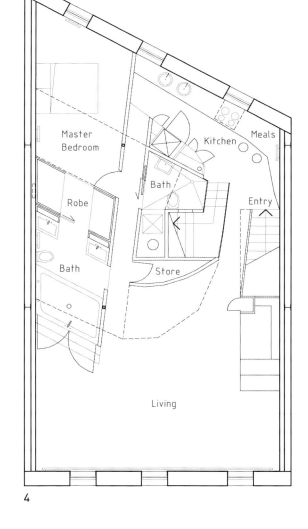

4

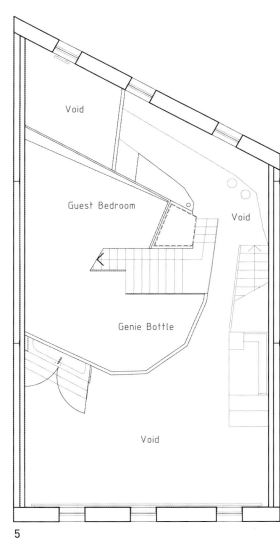

5

3

1 Mezzanine
2 Entry with perforated gold door
3 Street context
4 Level one floor plan
5 Mezzanine floor plan

6

7

6   Main bedroom
7   Kitchen
8   Bathroom
9   Living
10   Staircase landing

Photography: John Gollings, Gollings Photography

9

8

10

1

2

3

4

CITY BEACH HOUSE

CROUDACE ARCHITECTS

The brief was for a single-storey, modern home for a young family that is keen on entertaining. The unusually shaped site became a generator for the design, and the idea of spreading the house across the block evolved. One notion was to surround the house with garden so that from any room one could see garden on more than one side. Six separate outdoor courtyards resulted, all with different feels, providing a variety of outdoor living spaces. • Because the site dropped away from the road, the front end of the site was raised, giving the single-storey building more height and more street presence. This also generated some opportunities by allowing a level change inside the house and also kept the garage below the street level, reducing its presence. • The notion of increasing privacy as one moves into the site generated further ideas. The feature limestone wall on the street façade partly screens the garage, provides a notional gateway and partial separation to the entry court and softens the approach with the use of natural material. The garage and master bedroom provided the next separating element between public and private space and this was a significant separation. Once beyond this point, one is completely separated from the street. • The children's bedroom wing provided the final separation between the main courtyard and the children's 'backyard cricket' lawn. The masonry frames in the large main courtyard provide a notion of enclosure for the outdoor eating areas. • Materials were kept simple. Unitex was considered a durable wall finish for the coastal location; cedar lining was used under the eaves to provide some warmth in tone, where it would not be prone to weathering. Compressed fibre cement sheeting as a wall material under the roof and set back from the masonry below, enhances the floating roof plane concept.

5

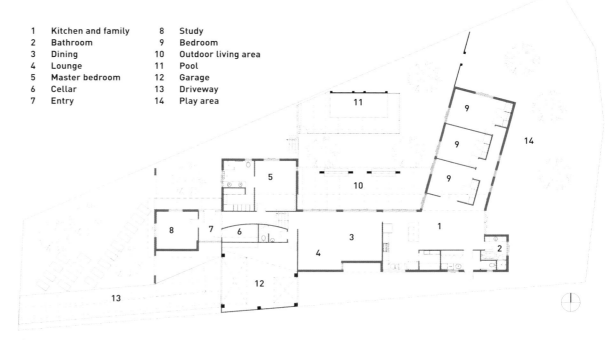

1	Kitchen and family	8	Study
2	Bathroom	9	Bedroom
3	Dining	10	Outdoor living area
4	Lounge	11	Pool
5	Master bedroom	12	Garage
6	Cellar	13	Driveway
7	Entry	14	Play area

1   Interior curved wall
2   Main courtyard frames
3   Street façade
4   Indoor/outdoor relationships
5   Family room and kitchen
6   Floor plan

Photography: Adrian Lambert. Acorn Photo Agency

6

1

2

CLARKE-MACLEOD HOUSE

BLIGH VOLLER NIELD

This house, in **Taringa, Queensland** is closely linked to the design and construction philosophies of California's 'Case Study' programme of the 1950s and 1960s, overlaid with today's concern for sustainable architecture. The Case Study programme included design based upon a standardisation of details, the use of prefabricated steel construction, and an emphasis on assembly techniques and construction details driving the visual outcome of the design. It is what Renzo Piano refers to as architecture created 'piece by piece' whereby the joy and finesse in detail determines a craft-like outcome. • The house takes standard, off-the-peg components such as pre-galvanised steel box sections to make the primary steel frame. However, these are thoughtfully detailed with internal bolted connections to create both the visual simplicity of mitred joints and a more durable solution where the welded and painted steel plates remain weather-tight and hidden within the steel box sections. Floor joists and roof purlins are made from galvanised tophat sections which are both lighter and stronger than timber and require a very basic form of fixing with power driven tek-screws into the primary steel frame (cleats and bolts were not needed). • The use of standard products pre-cut and assembled on site resulted in considerable economy with the steel frame constructed for around $10,000. The assembly process was so simple, and the frame so lightweight, that it was completed by two workmen over five days. Ironically, the builder and other workmen were carpenters by trade but found no difficulties in working with the various steel elements. • Apart from the steel framing elements, wall cladding, both internally and externally, consists of finely corrugated thin sheet steel materials pre-cut and pre-finished prior to assembly on site. The result is a high standard of finish and minimal time on site. The external cladding is left as a silver zincalume finish, whereas the interior wall and ceiling panels are pre-finished white with fine perforations to absorb sound and make a more liveable interior.

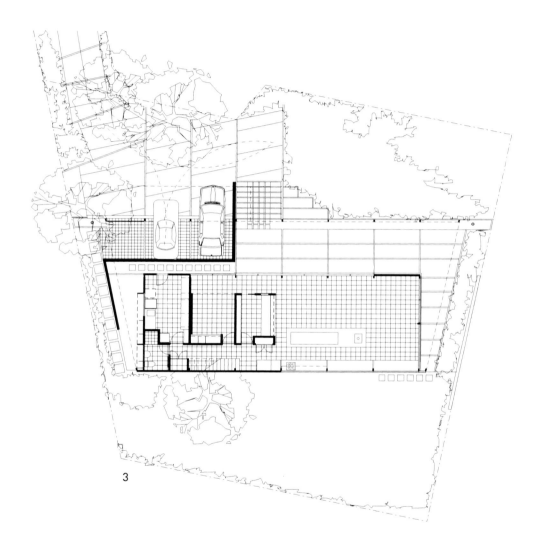

3

1 North-facing verandah space for outdoor living
2 Double-height interior living space
3 Site and ground floor plan

4

5

6

7

8

9

4   External dining area
5   East garden elevation
6   Night view highlights double-height living space
7   Stair constructed as stressed-skin box sections
8   Living area
9   Vertical proportions reflect those of surrounding trees

Photography: Jon Linkins

CONCRETE RESIDENCE

INARC ARCHITECTS

This 520-square-metre house uses the language of the cantilevered box forms of the surrounding **Studley Park** neighbourhood. These forms are cut into the site slope allowing views into the courtyard, as well as satisfying the clients' spatial requirements and minimising front elevation bulk. The middle level is aligned to maximise north light and to look towards the west; the topmost level provides views of **Melbourne**. • The house protects itself from the thermal environment by a highly insulated outer shell of concrete walls, roof and floors. To control heat loss and to minimise the requirement of internal blinds at night, double glazing was adopted throughout. External motorised blinds were installed to windows facing the east–west views, also providing privacy. • North-facing windows are shaded via cantilevered concrete eaves or by the offset floor above. The narrow shape of the rectangular building blocks, with external doors and windows on both sides of the building, allow for efficient cross-ventilation. • Green–grey concrete is used for the landscaping, walls and floor slabs, as well as the roofs that are covered in crushed bluestone rocks. The dark bronze metal components, glass, continuous external blinds and frameless balustrades form simple, serene planes that contrast with the tension created by the misalignment of the three levels and the placement of the top level on six slender columns. • The concrete used in this project had many functions: structure, waterproofing, thermal barrier and outer finished face. The aesthetic demands made of the concrete were probably the biggest departure from its standard commercial use. To visible faces, a green oxide pigment was added to temper the greyness. All visible edges were to be sharp right angles without the usual chamfer. Air bubbles in the outer face were encouraged in order to give the concrete the natural-looking random variation that is often associated with stone.

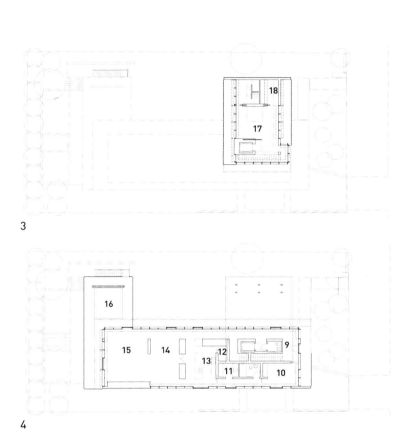

3

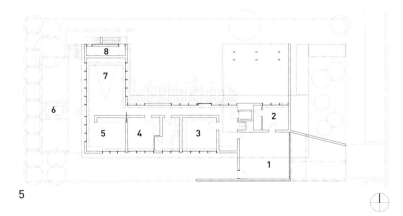

4

5

1	Garage
2	Workshop
3	Office
4	Bedroom 3
5	Art room
6	Spa
7	Media room
8	Plant room
9	Entry
10	Bedroom 2
11	Laundry
12	Store
13	Kitchen
14	Dining
15	Living
16	Terrace
17	Bedroom 1
18	Dressing room

Opposite:
Looking east from path within northern garden
2   Front elevation night view
3   Level three floor plan
4   Level two floor plan
5   Level one floor plan

2

Photography: Peter Clarke – Latitude Group

6

7

8

9

10

11

1

2

3

1   View from first-floor breezeway
2   Beach from first-floor deck
3   West courtyard with outdoor fireplace
4   Kitchen features granite bench top, jarrah cabinetry,
    coloured concrete floor
5   North elevation from beach
6   First-floor deck from north bedroom
7   First floor plan
8   Ground floor plan

**Photography: courtesy
Rachel Venables Design**

4

5

COROMANDEL HOUSE

RACHEL VENABLES DESIGN

This new beachfront home is on the **Coromandel Peninsula** on New Zealand's North Island. The clients' brief was for a holiday home that will become a permanent home when they retire. Sea views to the north and hill views to the southwest were a prime consideration. • The 'H' shape of the ground-floor plan was designed to create courtyards on each side of the central hall and gallery, which together with a long return verandah on the sea and north faces, provide a range of sheltered outdoor areas for varying weather conditions. The long low pitch of the roof recalls the New Zealand woolshed and the *whare nui* (Maori 'meeting house'), and is stylistically influenced by the Cape Cod beach houses of North America, and aspects of the New Zealand version of the Californian bungalow. • The upstairs wing incorporates bedrooms and a deck, with smaller decks off the two dormers to the bedrooms. The exterior is clad in painted cedar weatherboards, with Hinuera stone to the entry (bridging exterior and interior) and to the interior fireplace.

1	Entry
2	Bathroom
3	Bedroom
4	Bedroom
5	West courtyard
6	Living
7	Dining
8	Kitchen
9	Pantry
10	Bedroom
11	Surfboard storage
12	Service courtyard
13	Outdoor shower
14	Laundry
15	Hall
16	Bathroom
17	Bedroom
18	Terrace
19	Terrace
20	Bedroom
21	Terrace
22	Dressing

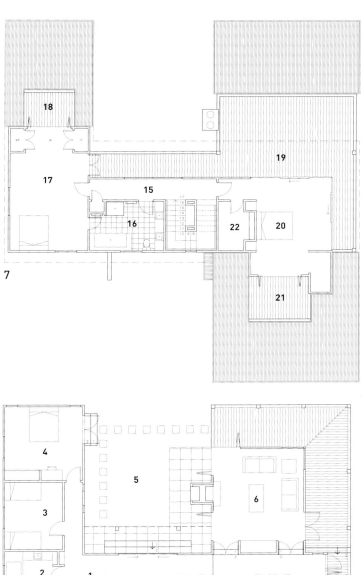

7

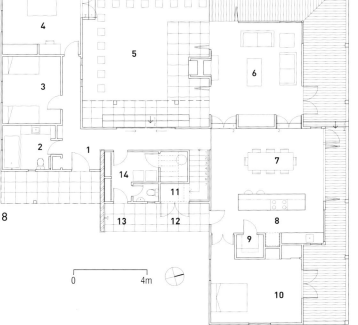

8

0   4m

6

75

COURTYARD HOUSE

UTZ-SANBY ARCHITECTS

The cliff-top site faces northeast and overlooks the **Pacific Ocean**. The views are dramatic and the proximity to the rock shelf and ocean below provides an ever-changing backdrop for the house. • The building was split into two pavilions, surrounding and enclosing a central courtyard, which then became the focal point for the design and a natural extension of the main living spaces. To reduce the overall bulk and height of the house some excavation was required to dig the lower pavilion into the slope of the site. Both pavilions have a solid base with a lighter construction for the second storey, which echoes a similar vernacular in the area. • The two pavilions are linked by a single circulation spine, defined by a masonry wall running the entire length of the house. The wall rises out of the landscaping and directs visitors towards the entrance door, through the courtyard link to the main living pavilion beyond. • Natural materials such as the recycled hardwood doors, and western red cedar cladding were chosen to complement the informal atmosphere of the house and as a reference to the traditional beach house aesthetic prevalent in the area. The courtyard, living room and terrace are all paved with natural limestone so that the transition from inside to outside is seamless. By limiting the amount of materials used, the courtyard remains a calm and uncluttered space. • The two large aerofoil roofs are important elements in the overall design. They appear to 'float' above the timber-clad pavilions. This was achieved by supporting the roof plane on eight columns, which are tied together at door head height by a steel ring beam. Above this, all four sides of the pavilion are glazed. This is accentuated at night when the roofs are up-lit from below.

2

Opposite:
    View of courtyard, looking through living pavilion to the horizon beyond
2   View from street, showing upper and lower pavilions
3   View from upper level bedrooms through living room to ocean view and rock shelf below

3

4

4   Looking through living room to courtyard with upper pavilion beyond
5   Detail of dining area and kitchen at the southern end of the room
6   Ensuite bathroom: all four ensuites are identical and can be completely opened to the bedroom and views
7   North elevation
8   View from entrance showing stair to lower level and link to the living pavilion adjoining the courtyard

Photography: Marian Riabic

5

6

7

8

THE CRAY SHED

KOIA ARCHITECTS

What are the components of a perfect holiday home? Ample room for friends and family to congregate, and large, sheltered outdoor living spaces are at the top of most lists. So it was with The Cray Shed, a 400-square-metre holiday home at **Pauanui**, on the beautiful **Coromandel Peninsula**. A south-facing building site close to its neighbours, and the requirement that the house be large enough for two families to enjoy, posed some interesting challenges. • The solution was inspired by the simple shape of a boatshed, reflecting its waterfront location. It presents a secure face to the street, with the living spaces opening towards the canal. Full-height sliding doors offer views through the house and out over the water, admitting lots of light into the home despite its difficult orientation. Another key feature is the double-sided open fireplace, allowing visibility to and from the canal. A big enclosed courtyard, again with an open fireplace, is tailor-made for entertaining al fresco. Wrapped around on three sides by the house, and with a high wall closing off the fourth side, it offers peace, privacy and protection from the prevailing southerly wind.

2

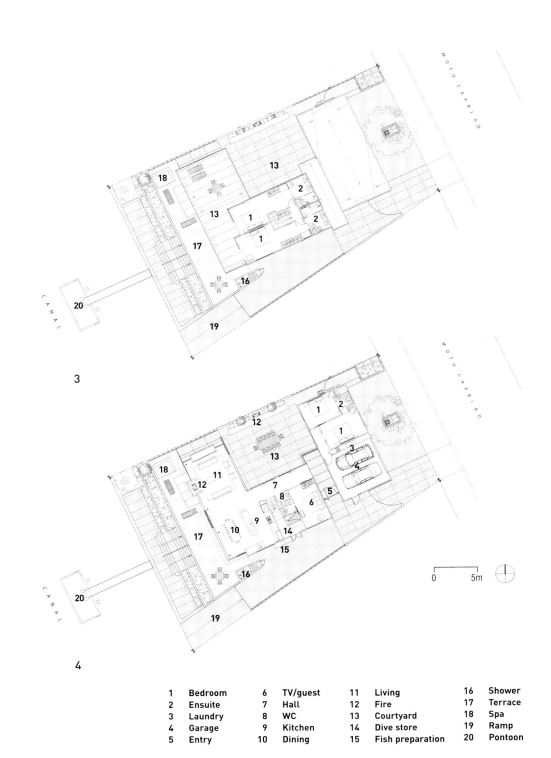

3

4

Opposite:
Landscaping is planned as a number of planted and hard surfaced terraces allowing for generous entertainment areas and the occasional high tide

2   View from canal
3   First floor plan
4   Ground floor plan

1	Bedroom	6	TV/guest	11	Living	16	Shower
2	Ensuite	7	Hall	12	Fire	17	Terrace
3	Laundry	8	WC	13	Courtyard	18	Spa
4	Garage	9	Kitchen	14	Dive store	19	Ramp
5	Entry	10	Dining	15	Fish preparation	20	Pontoon

5

6

7

5   The double-sided fire is enjoyable whether sitting inside or out
6   The sunny, sheltered courtyard provides a spot for year-round entertainment
7   The living room is transparent to allow maximum views of the canal
8   Retractable doors to both sides create a tent-like living area
9   Cosy living
10   Indoor entertainment

Photography: Kallan MacLeod; photographs provided courtesy of Trends Publishing International

8

9

10

CREMORNE STREET HOUSE

STEVENS LAWSON ARCHITECTS

This 470-square-metre family home is situated on a quiet street in the **inner Auckland suburb of Herne Bay**. Honed concrete blocks, dark stained timber and white precast concrete have been combined in an intensive sculptural composition that has a sense of permanence and craft. The cast concrete façade acts simultaneously as a public sculpture, a gift to the street, and as a protective mask for the private spaces behind • The living spaces are laid out in a linear progression along the length of the site, connecting the front courtyard to the back yard. This continuous space steps down several levels, following the natural slope of the land, defining distinct living and dining areas. The three bedrooms are on the upper floor along with the 'sky lounge', with views over the harbour. The sky lounge can function as a private living space with separate stair access, or as an extension to the main bedroom suite. • Shapes and textures are contrasted and repeated throughout the house and landscape, creating a sense of harmony, complexity and visual delight. The triangular geometries repeated throughout establish an integrated theme that engenders a personal character to the house.

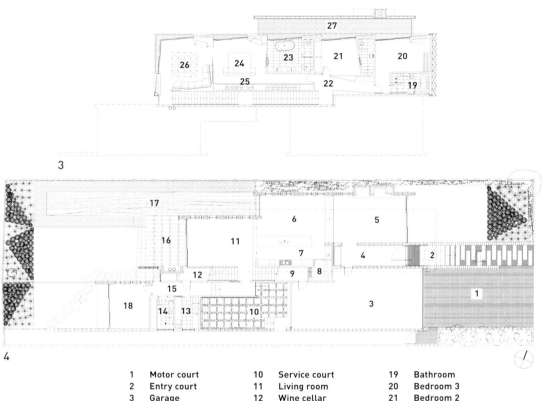

3

4

1	Motor court	10	Service court	19	Bathroom
2	Entry court	11	Living room	20	Bedroom 3
3	Garage	12	Wine cellar	21	Bedroom 2
4	Entry	13	Laundry	22	Hallway
5	Lounge	14	Bathroom	23	Ensuite
6	Dining room	15	Hallway	24	Master bedroom
7	Kitchen	16	Terrace	25	Dressing
8	Pantry	17	Pool	26	Sky lounge
9	Store	18	Study/guest room	27	Terrace

2

Opposite:
    View from front yard at night

2   View towards living spaces with sky lounge above

3   First floor plan

4   Ground floor plan

5   Kitchen area with living beyond
6   Main bedroom, dressing and ensuite area
7   The main ensuite, bedroom and sky
       lounge connect together
8   View of house from courtyard off study
9   Kitchen and dining area with living and
       pool beyond

Photography: Mark Smith

5

6

7

8

1

2

3

4

CUMBERLAND PARK RESIDENCE

STUDIO 9 ARCHITECTS

The client requested a renovation and addition to this Art Deco bungalow in the **Adelaide suburbs**. The brief was to address a modern, family-oriented lifestyle, providing flexible living spaces, access to light, and a flow from indoors to outdoors. • The existing house was a series of enclosed box-like rooms with poor, indirect access to the north-facing backyard. This portion of the house was turned over to the sleeping containers. The central corridor separates the children's area from the parents' suite, which incorporates a study/reading area and ensuite off the main bedroom. The children's bedrooms and bathroom were renovated. • The addition was intended to provide a contrast to the existing series of rooms. The modernist pavilion has a strong linear axis leading from the old to new, and utilises different volumes for different functions. The living and dining areas have a skillion roof, springing off the masonry wall providing volume and top light; these spaces are designed for enjoying life and entertaining family and friends in meals and celebration. The horizontal qualities of the kitchen suggest retreat, a place for the focused activity of food preparation. • During the design process, passive solar techniques were acknowledged. Roof overhangs at the higher level and the balanced bulkhead/verandah and pergolas limit sun penetration on the lower-level glass during summer and the shoulder seasons. Durable materials, seen as a positive sustainability principle, were selected. Windows and skylights allow a high level of light gain, reducing the reliance upon artificial lighting. Operable sashes allow a high level of ventilation, with the notion of creating front to rear air circulation. The pitched roof has a reflective surface and is angled away from the west to reduce solar heat gain.

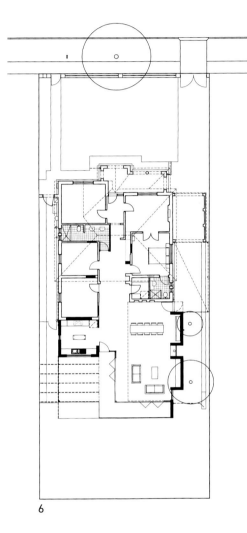

6

7

5

1   Night view of principal pavilion
2   Dining terrace and living area linked by folding doors
3   Kitchen
4   Bulkhead linking new to existing and indoor to outdoor
5   External view of principal pavilion and dining terrace
6   Floor plan indicating new works from existing
7   Timber floor in renovated bathroom was part of the original hallway

Photography: Sarah Long Photography

1

1   Bifold doors link family room to pool
2   Front façade is a collection of box-like forms
3   Ground floor plan
4   First floor plan

DALMAN HOUSE

DALMAN ARCHITECTURE

This 350-square-metre home for an architect and his family is located in **Papanui, Christchurch**. This site is close to town and is large enough to accommodate a tennis court and play areas for growing children. The court fits perfectly along the northeast boundary and was one of the reasons the section was purchased. With the tennis court position decided, the house itself was pushed as far as possible to the southern corner so that it maximised the northern outdoor living areas. • The plan of the house forms a cross on the site. The main axis consists of the main entry alongside the living room with a garage and shed to one side, and the family room with kitchen to the other. It is split by the other axis consisting of the walled courtyard and living room. The main circulation is located where the two axes cross. Sleeping areas have been located upstairs with separate wings for children and adults. • The living room was orientated towards one of the few landmarks in the area – a stand of very tall poplars which unfortunately have subsequently been cut down. It opens up to views through each end, and the side window provides views to a long grouping of deciduous trees which is one of the key aspects of the area. The overhang acts as a high-level verandah. • The construction is essentially two honed concrete block boxes, with a zincalume-clad central wing and bedroom container insertions into these boxes. The roof is butynol on insulated panel. Concrete floors throughout the ground floor provide a practical and cost-effective floor finish. • The styling is deliberately modernist but not minimalist. This is a family house that needs to be practical for growing children. While most walls are white, splashes of colour are provided by bright artwork, rugs and some highlighted wall finishes.

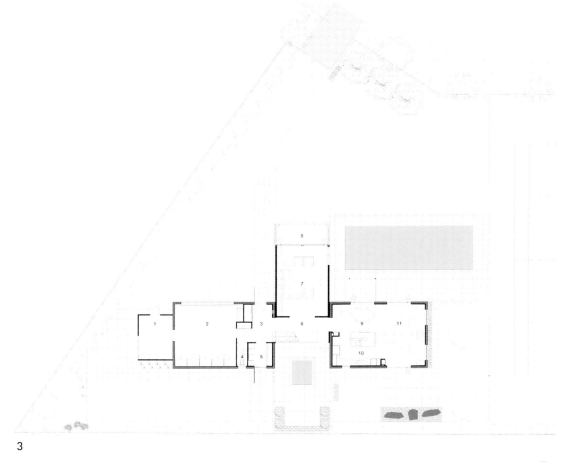

3

0   3m

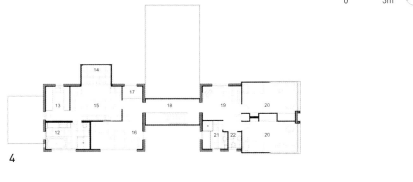

4

2

1	Shed	12	Ensuite
2	Garage	13	Dressing room
3	Entry	14	Balcony
4	WC	15	Master bedroom
5	Laundry	16	Study
6	Gallery	17	Void
7	Living	18	Gallery
8	Terrace	19	Kids' living
9	Dining	20	Bedroom
10	Kitchen	21	Bathroom
11	Family living	22	WC

5

6

7

5   Family room with children's bedrooms above
6   Artwork and a blue rug provide colour to the living room
7   Zincalume bedroom containers float above the family room and pool
8   Family room incorporates a black granite kitchen
9   Walled courtyard looking through the gallery
10 Entrance court with master bedroom balcony floating above

Photography: Patrick Reynolds

9

8

10

1

2

3

4

DRY HILLS HOUSE

ARCHITECTURE WORKSHOP

This house is situated on the outskirts of **Blenheim**, at the foot of the Withers dryhills. The long gable and faded cedar façade is the architects' man-made attempt to integrate with this local landscape. The envelope looks at combining the principles of rainscreen with an insulated thermal mass. The aim was to explore whether the climate could be controlled with the envelope rather than rely on an additional shade structure such as a verandah. A larger, more defined outdoor room, overlapping with kitchen, dining and the formal living areas, is enclosed by the roof and the rainscreen wall and supports outdoor living away from the prevailing wind. • The client wanted a bagged blockwork finish, coloured to match the hills and the coloured insitu concrete floor. The resulting freestanding internal solid walls, on the major longitudinal gridlines of the house, also continue into the landscape. The roof loads are supported on the blockwork by a ply-clad insulated timber frame. • The western red cedar exterior rainscreen reduces the weather load, protects the inner layer from the effects of strong sunlight and forms a cocoon of calmer air around the house that also assists insulation. It also shades the clerestory windows, reducing the heat gain while still allowing a filtered high light into the interior. • The exposed concrete blockwork, set to a 2.2-metre datum throughout, acts as a thermal flywheel, reducing the daily heat peaks and re-radiating this energy at night. Hopper-hung windows at the gable peaks are operable, allowing cross-ventilation at a high level. • The sliding doors with cedar shutters are detailed to fit in the cavity between the heavy and lighter layers. The 400-millimetre wall thickness adds a pleasing perception of protection to the occupants. From the outside, the house has a more ethereal, less solid presence in the dry landscape.

5

1   Overlapping gable roofs
2   Diagonal view from living to dining
3   North side outdoor room
4   Elevation against dry hills shows a more ethereal presence in the landscape
5   Central gallery
6   Bathroom interior

6

7

8

7   Western view against the dry hills
8   Filtered light through the clerestory windows
9   Eastern opening to kitchen/dining
10   External fireplace to outdoor room with formal living beyond
11   Outdoor room looking east

Photography: Stephen Goodenough

9

11

10

1

2

EAST MELBOURNE RESIDENCE

INARC ARCHITECTS

This three-level town house in **East Melbourne** was built in the early 1990s as an urban infill but suffered from poor design and sub-standard finishes. The building was divided into small rooms and lacked natural daylight in the ground-floor living areas. There was also a serious problem with heat gain from the east and west elevations during the summer. Access to the rear garden was via a single door at the end of a light well. On the positive side, the property boasted a good-sized rear garden and a double garage off a rear right-of-way. • The objective was to provide unimpeded views into the rear courtyard garden from the living areas. The kitchen has been relocated to the front of the house and the laundry has been moved to the basement/cellar. The courtyard garden has become an extension of the living space with a large sliding glass panel connecting the interior with the redesigned exterior. The clean open plan of the ground floor was achieved by supporting the southeast corner of the first and second storeys with a series of transfer beams. The first-storey floor of the original light well was removed to create the three-level, skylit atrium. • The installation of motorised external aluminium louvres has substantially cut down the heat load on the east and west elevations of the building. All the existing timber-framed windows were replaced with aluminium-framed, double-glazed units. This promotes heat retention in winter and also significantly reduces the ambient traffic and city noise. The ground floor polished bluestone floor acts as a heat sink in the winter when exposed to the morning sun and also acts as a unifying element over the three changes of level from the front entry door to the rear sitting area.

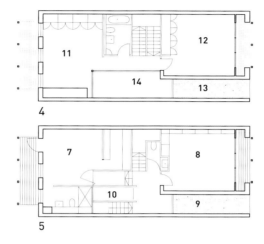

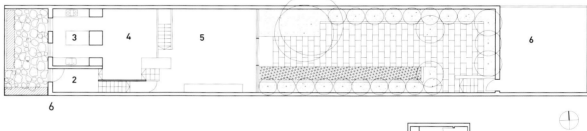

1	Laundry
2	Entry
3	Kitchen
4	Dining
5	Living
6	Garage
7	Master bedroom
8	Study
9	Roof
10	Void
11	Office
12	Bedroom
13	Roof
14	Void

1	West elevation
2	Rear courtyard garden
3	Living area with garden beyond
4	Second floor plan
5	First floor plan
6	Ground floor plan
7	Basement floor plan

8

9

10

11

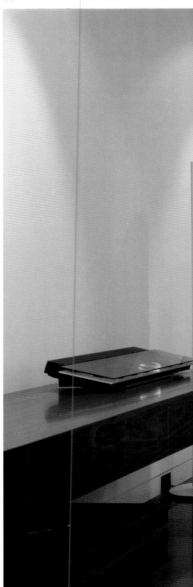

12

Photography: Peter Clarke – Latitude Group

13

1

2

3

FLORIDA BEACH HOUSE

ODDEN RODRIGUES ARCHITECTS

This was one of those rare occasions when clients consult their architect about the purchase of a property. And it was also one of the best 'finds' in **Western Australia's** vast continuum of 'beachside' suburb developments. • The property has its long side boundary providing northern orientation over public open space, natural dunes and the sea to the west, and is at the end of a cul de sac. • A condition of purchase was the requirement that the building be single-storey – to preserve the views of the properties behind – with a minimum 20-degree pitched roof. • The 230-square-metre house was constructed using conventional and economical materials. A polished concrete floor throughout provides a surface that is both aesthetically interesting and easy to maintain, and is the only concession to luxury. • A series of reconstituted limestone block piers stretch along the northern façade. Sliding past the front of the limestone blocks are seven large aluminium-framed glass doors, which can be opened to take full advantage of the cool ocean winds, bringing the outside world in and opening the inside out towards the beach. • The extensive glazed wall to the west, protected by its 6-metre-deep verandah, allows the living area to be intimately connected with its surroundings and magnificent views of the evening sunset. • Appropriate overhangs to the eaves keep out the unwanted summer sun, while the thermal mass and excellent wall-to-opening ratio result in an internal climate that is comfortable all year round.

4

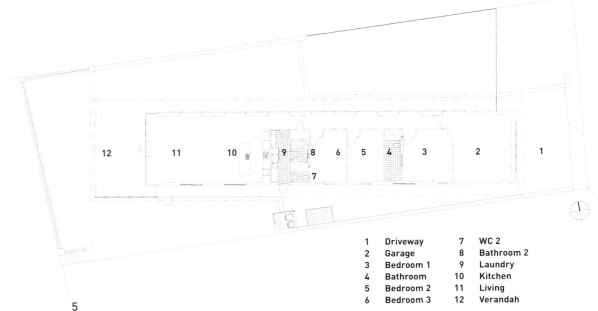

5

1   View across deck to ocean
2   Aspect from top of dunes
3   Looking west towards the verandah and ocean
4   North elevation
5   Site and floor plan

1	Driveway	7	WC 2
2	Garage	8	Bathroom 2
3	Bedroom 1	9	Laundry
4	Bathroom	10	Kitchen
5	Bedroom 2	11	Living
6	Bedroom 3	12	Verandah

6

8

7

9

10

6   Living area at night
7   Aspect from entry gate
8   Living area
9   View to kitchen from outside
10 Looking north towards the dunes

Photography: Robert Frith, Acorn Photo Agency

FOLDED HOUSE

DALE JONES-EVANS PTY LTD ARCHITECTURE

By critically editing and dismembering parts of an (unlisted) historic residence and outbuilding, the remaining space between the two existing styles of architecture allowed for the careful insertion of a new form. On this large, hillside site in a **beachside suburb of Sydney** a new origami-like architecture emerges as the calculated placement generates a web of inside–outside spaces and knits together a coherent plan for a new residence. • The existing historic Victorian/Italianate and Federation architecture is pruned right back to essentials, the external architecture proudly restored and the internal workings deliberately made moderne. The 1920's verandah wings are reconfigured at their southern corners and new translucent bookends housing wet areas symmetrically reframe a newly revealed and imposing view of the historic residence at the rear. • At this junction, a new architecture emerges: a copper-clad, folded, origami-like growth out of, into and between the existing modified structures. A linear perimeter plan encases a curvaceous internal plan, which wraps into and anchors the kitchen. A series of calculated external geometric folds radiate to form a hard shell while the belly of ceilings drip and flow to form a new dynamic internal space. The folded architectural form responds to climate: north is an open, extended eave, west is low, deep and uses an extended blade wall to control sun, while south is low and thick – a cut-out to prevailing weather. The folds make dynamic sculptural movements. • The new architecture acts as living hub – the former historic residence houses sleeping and bathing and the outbuilding comprises play space and a garage. The new external spaces are critical to the composition, from a green formal avenue at the entry, through two courts nestled between the built forms, one a garden the other a pool terrace and out to the back yard.

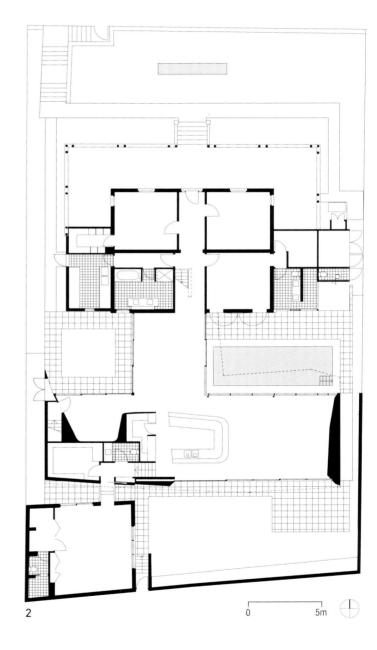

2

0   5m

3

4

5

6

3   View from dining room to pool court showing folds and curvature
4   View through stair
5   View from living room to kitchen
6   Northeast elevation across pool court at dusk

Photography: Paul Gosney (1,6); Trevor Mein (3–5)

1

1   Detail of interior forms
2   Front door entry
3   Exterior view of house illustrating folding elements
4   Floor plan

2

FOLDING HOUSE

STEPHEN JOLSON ARCHITECT

The Folding House is a 300-square-metre family home located in the **Melbourne suburb of Toorak**. The house is a series of three folding planes that wrap into each other. Each folding plane contains a different zone within the house: living, sleeping and garage. The exterior sculptural wrapping quality of the house is extruded throughout the interior. The interior ceiling spaces are articulated by these folding elements. • The house is designed around a large north-facing courtyard, which also provides a buffer between the sleeping quarters. Natural light is filtered throughout the house at all times of the day. The folding elements provide the separation between zones, negating the need for corridors.

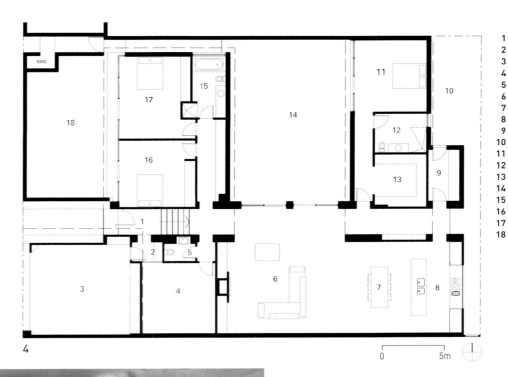

1	**Entry**
2	**Cloak**
3	**Garage**
4	**Study**
5	**Powder room**
6	**Living**
7	**Meals**
8	**Kitchen**
9	**Laundry**
10	**Service court**
11	**Master bedroom**
12	**Ensuite**
13	**Dressing room**
14	**Courtyard garden**
15	**Bathroom**
16	**Bedroom 2**
17	**Bedroom 3**
18	**Front garden**

4

0   5m

3

5

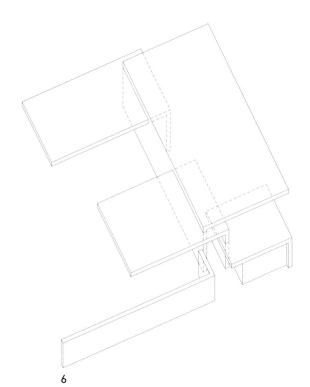

6

7

8

9

5   Folding elements extruded into interior
6   Axonometric
7   Open kitchen with glass splash-back as window into giant bamboo garden
8   View from family room across to open kitchen
9   Entry stairs

Photography: Scott Newett

1

2

1   West façade
2   Street side front entrance and large garden pool
3   View from river side
4   Ground floor plan

FORDHAM/JENKIN HOUSE

DESIGNINC PERTH PTY LTD

This new residence is located at **Minim Cove**, a development on the northern banks of the Swan River, about 15 kilometres **southwest of Perth** and within 5 kilometres of Fremantle. The three-level, 510-square-metre house was designed to maximise the panoramic and elevated river views and to comply with the local council's stringent height limitation of 8 metres above the ground floor podium level. • These requirements have resulted in a built form with a low-level horizontal aesthetic and an irregular 'H' plan, angled towards the river with extensive glazed areas, high volumes and large timber decks and cantilevered balconies. This configuration enables most areas in the house to enjoy the panoramic views. The visual ensemble from the street side is softer and more understated. • The horizontal tracery of the front timber slatted screen wall and entry gate open into a secluded environment. A large garden pool envelops the house and includes exotic carp, water lilies, stepping stones, timber decks, a water spout and two canyon-like rammed earth walls flanking the front entrance to the house. All this is set within a landscaped backdrop and is reminiscent of a Japanese garden – an oasis of peaceful tranquillity. • The central portion of the plan at ground level contains the living, dining and kitchen, designed as a double-volume space opening out onto a large timber terrace overlooking the river. This space is sheltered by a large roof overhead and a column-free structure ensures unimpeded views. • The lower ground floor houses a large undercroft space with provision for four cars. Again, there is no column structure to impede cars coming or going. A laundry, drying court and a storage/gymnasium area are also contained on this level. • The first floor contains two bedrooms and associated bathrooms on each wing. The central portion of the 'H' is a double-volume space extending to the ground floor and beyond to the spectacular view across the river.

3

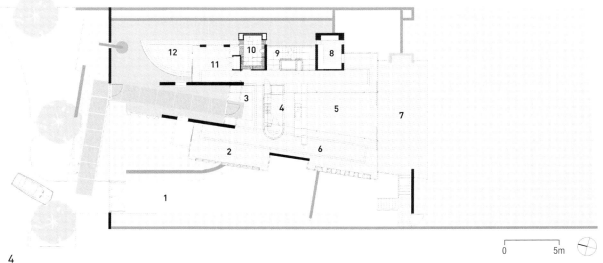

4

1 Driveway
2 Family room
3 Entry
4 Kitchen
5 Living
6 Dining
7 Terrace
8 Library
9 Stairs
10 Ensuite
11 Guest bedroom
12 Deck

0   5m

5

6

5   Ground floor main living space
6   Street side front entrance
7   Panoramic view of Swan River from main living space

Photography: Acorn Photo Agency

7

1

2

3

FORT DORSET HOUSE

HERRIOT + MELHUISH ARCHITECTURE

The main requirements of the brief were to create a comfortable, warm, family home that was good for entertaining while simultaneously making the most of the north-facing site. The challenges were the steep, sandy topography, the exposure to the wind, the client's desire for open-plan living with maximum connection between the interior and exterior, and the lack of built context. This 330-square-metre house was one of the first in a dense subdivision in the **Seatoun, Wellington**. • The resulting house is a composition of simple geometric forms inserted into the hillside and held together by the strong horizontal roof plane. Solid cement sheet forms with punched glazed openings address the neighbouring sites. These forms latch onto the more weighty and earthbound plastered concrete blockwork walls. The remainder of the house is a lighter exposed steel structure with large glazed walls. • The living spaces and bedrooms are elevated to make the most of the views. This also allows an internal connection from the garage to the entry, a specific request from the client. On level one, where the house cuts into the slope, a crib wall has been used to carve out a sheltered courtyard to the rear of the kitchen and living spaces. This results in glazing on three sides of the spaces, keeping the house locked into the site while preventing it from becoming buried. • An important factor for the interior was the relationship of the living spaces. From the kitchen, the client requested a visual connection with the family room, dining room and lounge. The lounge is connected to the family room by a bridge over the entry. To create a more formal entertaining space a large concealed sliding panel can be used to close off the lounge.

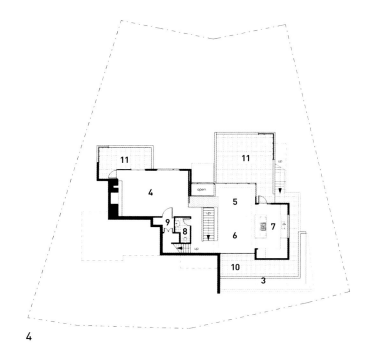

4

1   Garage
2   Entry
3   Planter
4   Lounge
5   Family room
6   Dining room
7   Kitchen
8   Bathroom
9   Cupboard
10 Courtyard
11 Terrace

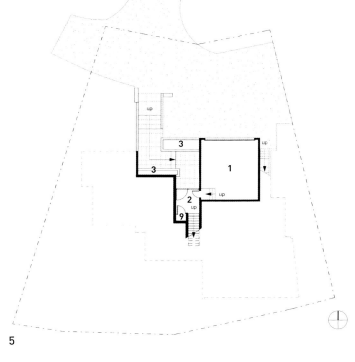

1   The house steps up the sloped site, creating terraces connected to the main living spaces
2   Expansive ocean views from top of entry stair through the family room
3   The house is a composition of simple geometric forms inserted into the hillside and held together by the strong horizontal roof plane
4   Level one plan
5   Ground level plan

5

6

6   Entry with bridge to lounge over
7   Main bathroom with lacquered joinery unit housing light box
8   Open plan kitchen, family room and dining room with
        sheltered courtyard to the south and terrace to the north
9   View across bridge connecting family room to lounge
10   Jarrah strip flooring and English tawa veneer panelling to
        entrance stair

Photography: Ian Robertson

7

8

9

10

FOSSIL COVE HOUSE

PRESTON LANE ARCHITECTS PTY LTD

This 180-square-metre home is set on 5 acres of bushland at **Tinderbox**, 20 minutes' drive **south of Hobart** on a site that overlooks native treetops and the Derwent River beyond. The client's brief included the need for separation between the living and the sleeping areas, maximum views, shelter from the roadway to the south, adherence to a modest budget and the accommodation of future needs. These needs informed the building's siting, form and concept. • The building is sited on a cleared area at the top of the slope, maximising views to the north and allowing the entry and the rear of the building to address the roadway. A layering of contrasting materials – warm natural timber boards and cold masonry walls – identify and soften the entry area, while combined they act as a barrier to the roadway. • The main living area has an open feel, with spaces separated and defined through different overhead ceiling planes and the varying depth of threshold conditions to the outside. From the sitting area, focus is drawn to the landscape and views beyond, but there is also a sense of containment. The adjacent dining area opens onto the deck. The kitchen overlooks the main living areas. • The bedrooms are housed over two split levels and are connected to the living space by an amenities link. Splitting these levels from the main level of the building creates a closer physical and more importantly psychological connection between the two. • The building accommodates the ever-changing Tasmanian climate through form, orientation and detail at the glazed ends. Its narrow modular arrangement of simple forms allows for all living spaces to face north and circulation spaces to run along the south, ensuring deep solar penetration during the winter months and easily controlled heat gain during the warmer months, providing a naturally comfortable and energy efficient house in a moderately cool climate.

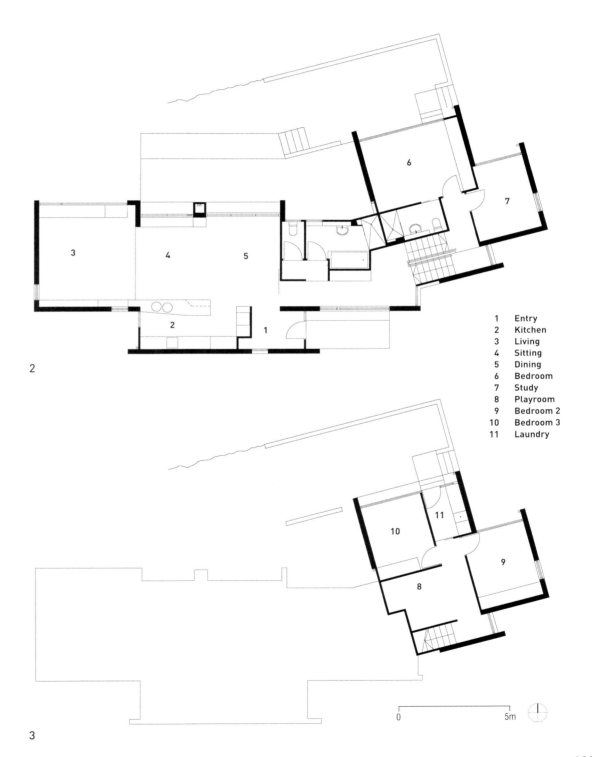

1	Entry
2	Kitchen
3	Living
4	Sitting
5	Dining
6	Bedroom
7	Study
8	Playroom
9	Bedroom 2
10	Bedroom 3
11	Laundry

Opposite
    External view towards living areas from bedroom wing
2   Main level floor plan
3   Lower level floor plan

0   5m

4

4   North elevation
5   View from deck along north face of building
6   Interior view from living area
7   View from circulation corridor towards main living spaces
8   View from deck through timber box seat to kitchen beyond
Photography: Richard Eastwood

5

6

7

8

1

1   View from northeast
2   View from east
3   Courtyard
4   Bathroom

Photography: Richard Glover

FUTURE HOUSE

INNOVARCHI

The timber house was designed for the Year of the Built Environment *Houses of the Future* exhibition, first held in the forecourt of the Sydney Opera House and ending with a permanent exhibition at Sydney's Olympic Park. • The house explores the single-family dwelling and its relationship with the environment. It showcases a 'fully integrated ESD solution', incorporating some of the most up-to-date technologies to deliver a home that is comfortable to live in and provides a sustainable housing option for the future. • The house introduces innovative features in three main areas: water management, solar systems and heating/cooling systems. • The house is designed so that the surface area of the house in effect is its own water catchment, and storage is provided beneath the skin of the house in a bladder. Rainwater can be used in the house for all domestic uses, such as toilet flushing, in taps, in appliances, and if required, can be treated and made safely potable. • Two solar systems are featured in the house: a solar hot water heating system and solar panels. The solar hot water system is different from conventional solar systems, in that it uses cylindrical evacuated glass tubes to absorb the heat from the sun. The tubes maximise exposure to sun and result in a surface area that is always perpendicular to the sun. • The house incorporates Dye Solar Cells (DSC), which use a dye-based nano technology to harness solar energy from direct or indirect light sources. The system is biomimetic, and works by imitating the process of photosynthesis in plants. The performance characteristics of the DSC make it ideal for use on vertical surfaces, indoors or in shadowy conditions. • The house's innovative cooling and heating system uses two streams of airflow through the structure of the house to efficiently maintain comfortable temperatures for the living spaces. The system can best be described as actively controlled passive heating, cooling and ventilation.

2

3

4

1

2

3

4

5

GOLD COAST PENTHOUSE

SPACE CUBED ARCHITECTURE STUDIO

This **Gold Coast** penthouse apartment was a shameless example of 80's decadence: pink marble, pink granite, pink toilets, pink, pink, pink ... The architects proposed the removal and demolition of all finishes and fittings in the apartment and their replacement with a simple, elegant, contemporary design. • The clients were focused on achieving an apartment that was simple and full of light, and hoped to better capture and somehow 'magnify' the view. Much of their response was prompted by the negative spaces and drab finishes that had adorned the apartment, creating dull, lifeless, disproportionate spaces that seemed to distance the beachside apartment from its locality. • Many of the disjointed and obscure spaces, particularly in the living areas, needed to be rationalised to form a sense of spatial boundary. The problem of the main living area was simply solved with a raised platform, combined with some other minor elements that not only created a comfortable space but defined the spatial uses of the adjoining areas. Physical barriers between the individual spaces were removed and in some cases display casework was installed to delineate or screen the individual use areas. This created an overall impression of openness and visual attachment that further enveloped the views. • This design intention was carried through into the smaller spaces including bedrooms, ensuites, and powder rooms including the detailing that again allowed for the creation of an overall impression of openness and visual attachment and thus altering the perception of space and boundary. • Details and finishes were selected to not only lead the eye, but to define space and reflect light and colour to give depth and warmth where appropriate. Finishes were selected to stand the rigours of time and reflect the quality of the apartment.

1 Large spherical lights manipulate floor level and perceived height
2 Timber deck was raised to the existing level of the pool hob
3 By removing internal walls and expressing the curved form of the stair, the apartment is transformed into a procession of varying spaces
4 Existing unused 'niches' converted using display joinery
5 The detail in the new platforms/steps included 'hidden' lighting
6 Ensuite and walk-in-robe, reconfigured to allow direct access between each and views to the ocean from the spa
7 Master bedroom opens to the living void via an operable sliding glass wall and blinds

Photography: Brad Smith Photographics

6

7

HECKLER HOUSE

NOVAK & MIDDLETON ARCHITECTS

The house is located on an elevated site west of **Nelson**, overlooking Tasman Bay and back to Mount Arthur, on New Zealand's South Island. • The client brief called for a contemporary home that maximised the site's environment and stunning aspect. The house had to be easy to live in with a strong connection to the exterior. • The house is constructed on a single level and divided into two distinct forms, which incorporate the public and private areas. The public spaces, incorporating living, dining, kitchen and family areas, have been arranged adjacent to each other and are largely open-plan, interlinked by a gallery that forms a spine along the back of the house. The private spaces are accessed off a secondary gallery and provide more secluded and restful areas removed from the open plan environment. • The forms have been arranged to maximise morning sun to the bedroom areas and afternoon sun to the living spaces, as well as capturing the panoramic views. • The house forms a strong connection with its landscape through use of solid forms balanced by extensive glazing. The large floating roof, which appears to hover above the plaster portals, has a dual benefit of providing shade in the summer months and allowing cooling breezes to enter through the clerestory windows. • The use of solid forms together with expansive use of glass gives the sense of being close to the elements but protected from them at the same time. The house creates a sense of shelter in close connection with its environment.

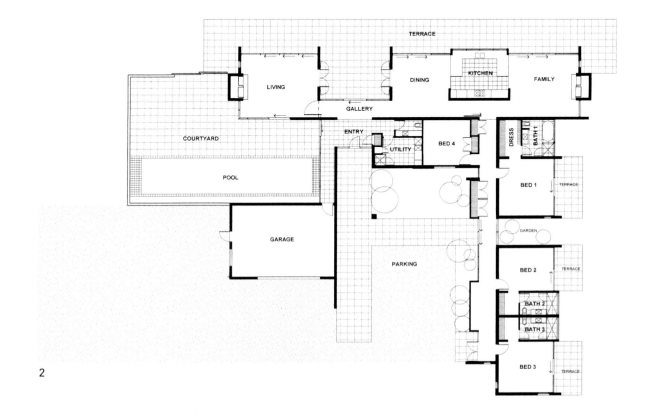

2

3

Opposite:
North terrace outside living room looking back to Nelson
2   Floor plan
3   An expansive house in an expansive landscape

4

5

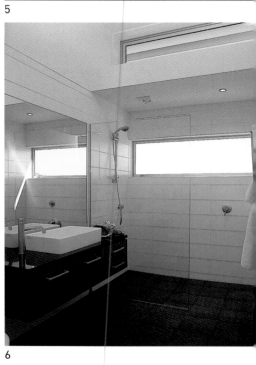

6

7

4   Large floating roofs hover above plaster portals with clerestory windows
5   View from main entry through to pool area
6   Guest bathroom
7   View from family space through to kitchen and dining
8   View across living terrace to Tasman Bay
9   Living terrace and pool

Photography: Elizabeth Goodall (p.130,5,7); Simon Novak (3,4,6.8.9)

8

9

1

2

3

HEDGES RESIDENCE

BAYDEN GODDARD DESIGN

The project is situated on one of the most **exclusive beachfront streets** in **Queensland**. The street contains an eclectic mix of architectural styles, forms and building typologies, ranging from single dwellings to highrise buildings. The street acts as a connection between local beach villages and carries large volumes of pedestrian and vehicular traffic. The site itself is a narrow beachfront lot with primary aspect towards the beach to the east. • The brief called for the design of a contemporary three-bedroom home with study and parking for four cars, that capitalised on the beachfront location and the excellent views to the east and southeast. The design needed to provide separate living spaces for children and consider environmental and site-specific issues such as corrosion and long-term building maintenance. • The approach was to create a design that turned its back on the busy street, resulting in a tranquil and dynamic interior that focused on the view towards the ocean. By locating the main entry in the centre of the site on the north side, the design was split into two pavilion-like elements. The first pavilion houses the children's bedrooms and rumpus, acting as a buffer to the street. The second pavilion contains the living spaces and master bedroom, opening to the beach and views beyond. • Locating the entry in the centre of the plan meant that it then became part of the living spaces, enhancing the feeling of interior space. The floating stair was introduced to this space, allowing the feeling of vertical and horizontal space to be maximised immediately upon entering the building. • Service areas have been compressed to the south and west, allowing the 616-square-metre house to open to the views to the east and light from the north. Small gill-like fenestration captures oblique south side views while protecting against weather and maximising privacy.

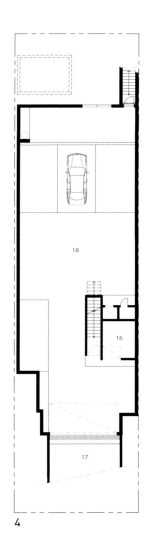

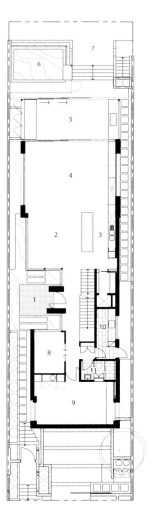

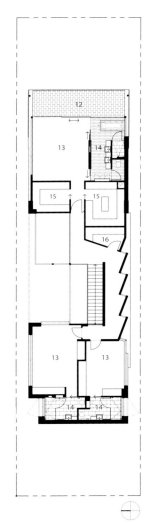

1   Entry courtyard
2   Dining
3   Kitchen
4   Living
5   Outdoor/indoor room
6   Pool
7   Private beach access
8   Study
9   Rumpus
10   Laundry
11   Bathroom
12   Balcony
13   Bedroom
14   Ensuite
15   Robe
16   Store
17   Driveway entry
18   Garage

1   Beachfront façade opens to capture maximum sunlight and beach views
2   This enclosable deck capitalises on beachfront entertaining and views
3   Entry courtyard allows the residence to breathe through its core
4   Floor plans from left: lower ground level, ground level, upper level

135

5

6

7

8

9

10

5   Open plan living and dining spaces open directly to beachfront views
6   Living spaces flow uninhibited to outdoor beach entertaining and views
7   Luxury master ensuite capitalises on beachfront views
8   The entry maximises vertical and horizontal spatial qualities
9   Extensive glazing draws desired light and ventilation into surrounding living spaces
10   Open plan living is enhanced by this centrally located kitchen

Photography: Mark Cranitch

1 A white glass panel behind the shower fills the internal bathroom with borrowed light from the sun-filled entry beyond
2 The white glass windows allow northern daylight in while maintaining privacy
3 Recycled karri stairs sit against a monolithic wall of unglazed mosaic tiles
4 The roof soars up to the north allowing in valuable winter sun; the eaves screen the harsh western and summer sun
5 Ground floor plan
6 First floor plan
7 Water tanks sit on the recycled jarrah deck, providing water pressure to taps below and screening neighbour's courtyard

Photography: Andrew Wuttke

2

1

3

HENRY HOUSE

BREATHE ARCHITECTURE

This project involves the addition of a second-storey extension, tucked well into the existing building. The roof rises from the existing southern wall, eliminating any overshadowing, and capturing valuable northern sunlight. The roof sails past a wall of translucent glass and is angled to allow winter sun in and to exclude summer sun. The stairwell, located in the centre of the ground floor, brings natural light from above deep into the previously dark ground floor. • The finishes were kept to a simple yet robust palette of materials. Recycled jarrah was selected for its beauty, durability and sustainability. Translucent white laminated glass provides superior thermal performance and can provide abundant natural light without overlooking neighbours. Galvanised steel cladding was chosen for its durability and compatibility with the semi-industrial architecture of the surroundings. • The house is designed to be a tough, simple little building giving light and privacy to those inside and unimposing beauty and simplicity to the wider community.

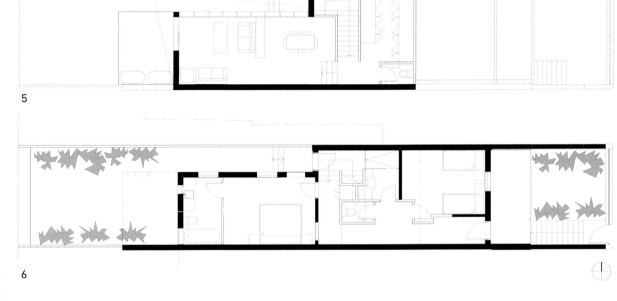

5

6

4

7

1

2

3

HOUSE AT CASTLECRAG

MONCKTON FYFE ARCHITECTURE AND INTERIORS

This 1952 building on **Sydney's North Shore** has been expanded and modified in close consultation with the original architect, Peter Muller. The original house is particularly unique in mid-20th-century Australian architecture, with its experimental qualities including a dynamic indoor/outdoor living relationship, strong cantilevering horizontal forms, snotted brickwork and tripartite zig-zag fascias. Although the influences of Frank Lloyd Wright exist in this house, Muller created a new Australian style of his own, utilising local materials and relating to the Australian landscape context. • The new interventions can be readily identified, being stylistically rooted in a more reductive Japanese aesthetic, complementary with Wright's philosophy. The strong horizontality of the original house is accentuated in the new work. The extruded plane of the cantilevered master suite extends the form and horizontality of the building in keeping with the rock platforms of the surrounding landscape. It also serves to provide an outdoor covered area. • The rear of the house has become more transparent to allow the 'living' part of the house to open up and capture the views. The seductive elements of light and shadow are now more readily available with the freeing up of the courtyard connections. • A new dark-tiled, wet-edge pool was designed to complement the connection of the building to its site, from the house through the landscaped rear yard and to the bush and harbour beyond. • Space is ordered and functional, re-composed within the existing fabric of the house to serve the family's needs and lifestyle. The planning has simplicity in composition, spatial sequencing, and either enclosure or transparency, depending on requirements. • The focus was to enhance the qualities of interaction of the building with its site and environment and to provide a sympathetic response to the existing built works.

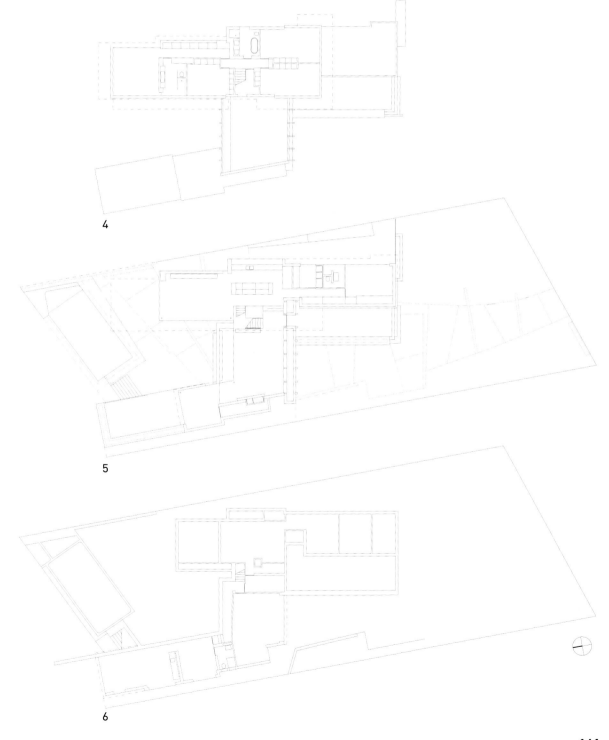

4

5

6

1   Cantilevered horizontal planes of the building float out over the pool
2   Irregular patterns follow into the landscape to continue the dynamic composition
3   Extruded planes express horizontal forms
4   First floor plan
5   Ground floor plan
6   Basement plan

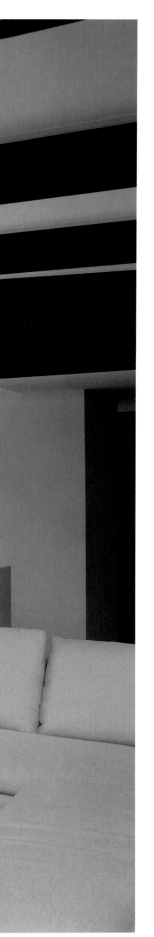

8

9

10

11

7   Living area across rear courtyard
8   Guest bathroom
9   Kitchen
10   Living area
11   Distant harbour views across pool

Photography: Michael Nicholson

1

HOUSE FOR I & A

BLIGH VOLLER NIELD

On a long narrow site with a western aspect to the **Brisbane River** at **Yeronga**, the house accommodates a family of four. The site enjoys a northern view over a large neighbouring garden. The house is one room wide and two storeys high with internal spaces aligned along the southern boundary and stepped down a slight slope towards the river on the west. Most rooms enjoy views of the river with a northern aspect to a large linear outdoor 'room' bordered by a lap pool on the northern boundary. • Of particular importance to the design is the integration of landscaping, extending from the entry down through the large outdoor room to the river. This space defines the house with views maintained from all rooms out into the generous void. It provides both a sense of spaciousness and luxury in contrast to the tight constraints of the site as well as allowing access to extended views, landscaping and the swimming pool. • A cost-effective construction was achieved by a conventional steel and timber stud frame, clad with rendered 'fibro'. Particular attention was given to the finishes and detailing to ensure a refined outcome, consistent with the client's brief and budget. Large areas of glazing are generally standard silver-powdercoated, aluminium-framed systems with carefully detailed aluminium screens providing privacy and protection from the sun.

2

1 North wall defines a large outdoor room along the full length of the house
2 Outdoor room has varying levels of enclosure and landscaping
3 Upper level floor plan
4 Lower level floor plan

1	Driveway	17	Shed
2	Garden	18	Balcony
3	Entry	19	Bedroom 1
4	Garage	20	Walk-in robe
5	Lounge	21	Wash room
6	Wine cellar	22	Bathroom 1
7	Powder room	23	Study
8	Laundry	24	Linen store
9	Kitchen	25	Bathroom 2
10	Living	26	WC
11	Upper courtyard	27	Void
12	Courtyard	28	Bedroom 2
13	Outdoor room	29	Bedroom 3
14	Pool	30	A/C store
15	Pool deck	31	Bedroom 4
16	Pergola		

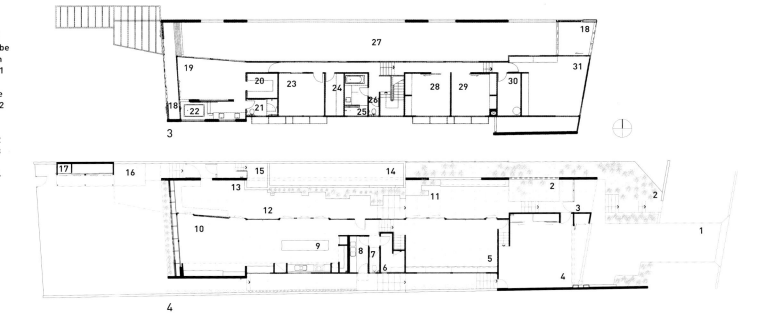

5

5   Kitchen and family room
6   Upper level bathroom 1
7   Swimming pool and outdoor room
8   Loggia outside family room with upper level balcony to master bedroom and screened view to west

Photography: David Sandison

6

7

8

1

2

1   Night view of northeast corner entry
2   West view from banks of Brisbane River
3   Southeast corner from the garden
4   Upper level floor plan
5   Lower level floor plan

HOUSE FOR S & P

BLIGH VOLLER NIELD

The site for this house enjoys an existing private jetty on the **Brisbane River** and the remnants of an established garden. The clients are a professional couple, with keen interests in both boating and gardening. Consequently, the brief was significantly influenced by the desire for the house to be both a garden pavilion and a boat house. • The house is sited in the centre of the corner block taking advantage of both the river view and large garden and pool to the northeast. An existing 'shed' adjacent to the river boundary has been retained and refurbished to allow the client a workshop to maintain and store his wooden boats. • The general planning arrangement consists of a Z-shaped, two-storey pavilion, one room wide, moving across the site. The relatively shallow plan enables the building to be opened to both the east and west ensuring strong visual links with the river from all parts of the site. This plan form also enables all rooms of the house at both levels to gain river glimpses. • The western façade has a second external folding wall with integral screening to counter the harsh afternoon sun. The combination of this wall and the floating upper floor creates a deeply recessed outdoor room at the ground level, which acts as a shelter for the internal living spaces. • Maintaining a strong link between the internal living spaces and the surrounding landscape was the foremost desire throughout the design process. The simple forms and materiality of the building reflect the desire to enhance the natural features of the site without being overly dominant. Combining off-white rendered surfaces and painted plasterboard with embellishments of natural timbers, the detailing is refined and direct, resulting in a sense of relaxation, informality and openness.

3

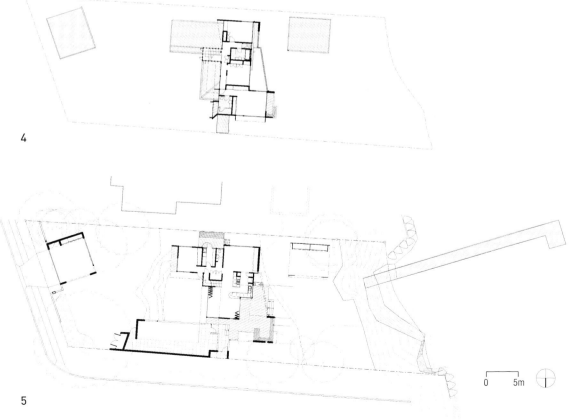

4

5

0   5m

Photography: David Sandison

7

6   8

9

10

11

1

2

3

HOUSE IN RICHMOND

JACKSON CLEMENTS BURROWS ARCHITECTS

This building very carefully attempts to make a positive and appropriate contribution to the immediate streetscape while demonstrating the value of highly considered contemporary architecture in **Melbourne's** sensitive heritage areas. • The project was an opportunity, a chance to repair an original double-fronted timber cottage that was a disregarded element of an important and predominantly heritage streetscape. An extension of the building form was required to accommodate an expansive brief – the result is an example of an architectural approach that complements and reinforces the surrounding heritage buildings through conscious contrast. • The original house form was preserved, enhanced by the removal of extensions and verandahs unsympathetic to the original architectural style. The new extension was conceived as an object within a garden – walls are dissolved and the garden itself becomes an extension of the living space. A glazed pavilion of protected living space is sheltered by an abstract upper form, enclosing bedrooms and associated program. • Visual bulk and associated overshadowing were minimised by centrally locating the highest form, tapering it back towards the southern end. A windowless façade of translucent cladding was devised on the east side to address overlooking while still providing natural light to the internal spaces. Lost trees were replaced by a natural and artificial garden. An operable glass louvred screen on the west façade, finished in varying tones of green film, mimics the texture of the leafy surrounds while diminishing the visual bulk and providing solar protection and privacy to the upper level bedrooms and neighbouring gardens. • The result is a combination of sheltered garden living spaces and private bedroom zones concealed within a highly considered abstract form.

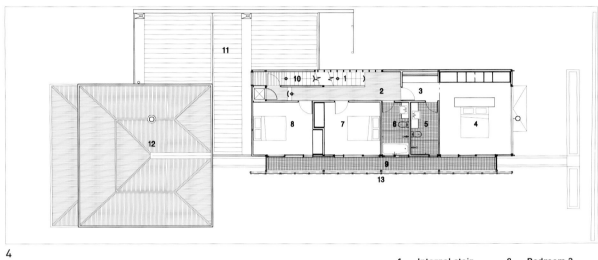

4

1	Internal stair	8	Bedroom 3
2	Hall	9	Western deck
3	Dressing area	10	External stairs
4	Master bedroom	11	Garage roof
5	Ensuite	12	Existing house roof
6	Bathroom	13	Operable louvre
7	Bedroom 2		screen

5

1	Driveway	9	Service yard
2	Entry	10	Kitchen
3	Retreat	11	Dining
4	Bedroom 4	12	Living
5	Ensuite	13	Entertaining deck
6	Study	14	Pond
7	Garage	15	Sunken garden
8	Laundry	16	Lawn

1   Streetscape
2   Garden living space
3   Rear extension with glazed west screen
4   First floor plan
5   Ground floor plan

6

7

8

9

10

6   Sunken garden
7   Kitchen
8   Relationship of kitchen to living area beyond
9   Master bedroom
10   Translucent wall to stairs

Photography: John Gollings, Gollings Photography Pty Ltd

1

2

3

HUSKER DU II

ELLEN WOOLLEY ARCHITECT

This house plays cheeky gymnastics with the site and within its volume. The battleaxe site is idyllic **Sydney** landscape: a sinuous sandstone cliff dropping northwards at nearly 45 degrees to native bushland and a harbour estuary. The cross-section of the house is a simple response: a cool grey barrel, with its back to the south, sits outwardly like a rock and internally like a cave. The barrel peels open towards the light and the bush, becoming a tree house, but the overt section as the house's first reading belies its depth and ongoing complexities. • The inherent dynamics in the site clearly inform the design of Husker Du II, for example the strong cross-section that moves from rock/cave to tree house. The effect on the house of ever-shifting elements like light and wind are also an obsession, with each face responding both externally and internally to the natural light it receives. • The split-level entryway rolls out informally from front door to back door, maintaining a strong link to the ground. Projections from the studio and the kitchen upstairs into the entry volume animate and welcome one further. The powerful curved section, with its shifting washes of strong daylight, makes the act of going up a delight. At the top, teetering over the precipice, northern openings slip away to provide generous and sheer window-seats amongst the treetops. • Within the large curved interior, the rooms stack up visually like large cubes. Colour, selected from the site, articulates these boxes with a sort of chiaroscuro effect. • Husker Du II maintains nature's equilibrium, respecting the existing native fauna and flora and the natural water movements. Rain pours freely off the south roof/wall onto bedrock and directly into little natural frog pond gullies in the rock and on to the bush creek below, caught on the north by a tank for reuse.

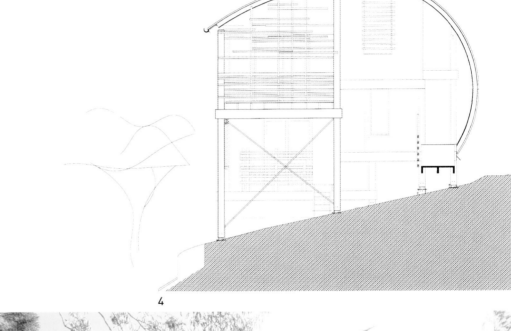

4

5

1   Entry volume
2   Kitchen
3   Front elevation
4   West elevation
5   Southeast view

Photography: Richard Glover Photography

1

2

3

JAMES-ROBERTSON HOUSE

DAWSON BROWN ARCHITECTURE

The site is on a steep, northeast-facing slope on the western foreshores of Pittwater to the north of **Sydney**, and is surrounded by the Ku-ring-gai National Park. • The house is a series of glass, steel and copper pavilions designed to blend into a stunning natural environment. The lower pavilions are grounded on a massive sandstone retaining wall excavated from the site and engineered to geotechnically stabilise the slope. Arrival involves a boat trip, beach walk and a slow hill climb to the enclosing rampart walls of the entry. • The sloping walls lead to the first-level bamboo grove with its study, guest bedroom and cellar, linked by the huge cantilevering floors of the pavilions above. • The path continues up past the copper-clad walls of the main double-height living pavilion to the original cliff face adorned with the hanging roots of a giant Port Jackson fig tree. It is here the fully transparent glass pavilions are revealed and the path continues past the louvred and meshed pantry to the central spine adjoining the kitchen/dining room. The space is covered by interlocking layers of steel hoods and copper roofs. • The main bedroom pavilion or eyrie sits 50 metres up the slope in a grove of casuarina trees accessed only by a frighteningly steep inclinator ride. • The interiors were all customised like a boat interior to maximise a sense of openness and efficiency. The crucial function of food storage (no easy access to a corner store) was a contemporary adaptation of the outback meat safe with a louvred screen scullery. Materials used include terrazzo basins and ash joinery throughout. • The project is a beautifully crafted contemporary building built in extreme and demanding circumstances where the technical details of construction are inseparable from the design process.

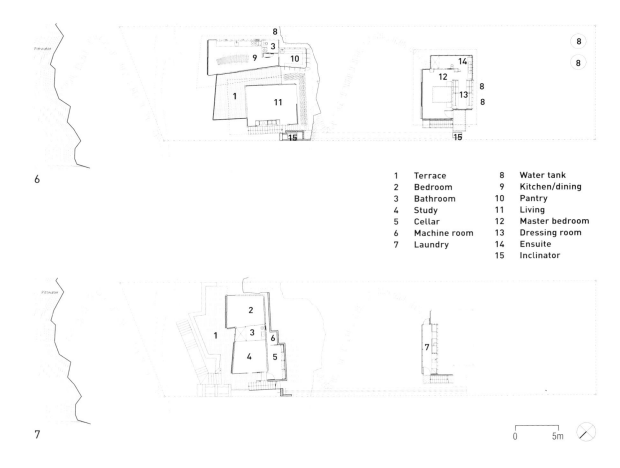

6

1	Terrace	8	Water tank
2	Bedroom	9	Kitchen/dining
3	Bathroom	10	Pantry
4	Study	11	Living
5	Cellar	12	Master bedroom
6	Machine room	13	Dressing room
7	Laundry	14	Ensuite
		15	Inclinator

7

0   5m

1   Curved Caroline Casey dining room table
2   Dining room
3   Pavilions from the water surrounded by National Park
4   Dining/kitchen viewed from deck overlooking ocean
5   Entry walkway with hanging fig tree
6   Upper floor plan
7   Lower floor plan

4

5

8

9

10

11

12

13

8   View from dining room to the deck featuring Caroline Casey 'Zella' day bed
9   Entry sandstone walls and cantilevering kitchen/dining pavilion
10   Dining room/kitchen with Caroline Casey table and hanging aboriginal fish trap
11   Living room pavilion
12   Living pavilion and views to Barrenjoey lighthouse
13   View through breezeway to the ocean

Photography: Anthony Browell (1–3,5,8–10,12)
Patrick Bingham-Hall (4,11,13)

1

2

3

4

5

KAPITI COAST BACH

BEVIN + SLESSOR ARCHITECTS

A bach existed on this site at **Paraparaumu** for some fifty years before succumbing to the elements. The site is a dramatic location, fronting the beach with direct views to Kapiti Island, and uninterrupted sunsets. The experience and memory of running down to the surf from the bach has continued through the generations of the Hawke's Bay family that owns the site. • The clients wanted to maintain this easy and relaxed experience with the new bach. Other requirements were to maintain privacy from the road, shelter, views and connection to the beach, with maximum opportunities for outdoor living. Materials needed to be robust, to withstand the westerlies and intense effects of the sun. The bach also needed to accommodate up to two families, and act as a temporary office when required. • The new bach wraps around a covered deck, which acts as an outdoor room. This space becomes the centre of the bach and the point from which other activities pivot. Timber louvres are utilised to provide cross-ventilation through the rooms while the windows remain as large openings. The floor area was kept to a minimum, allowing the budget to accommodate the higher quality materials and fixings required to withstand the elements. • The living space was designed as a single simple volume, containing a central dining table, kitchen bank at the end wall and sitting areas with an orientation towards the beach. The materials were kept to a very simple, robust palette, and include marine-grade aluminium cladding and windows, black-stained plywood and zinc-capped macrocarpa rafters with a clear finished plywood ceiling and particle board floor.

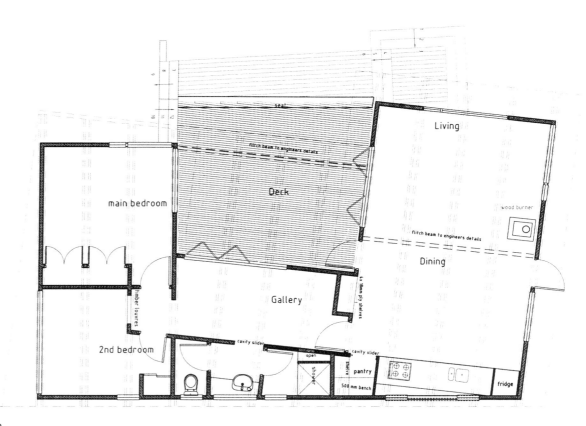

8

6

7

1   Arrival
2   Enclosed deck
3   Kitchen
4   Filtered light over deck
5   Living space
6   Street view
7   Deck view to beach
8   Floor plan

Photography: Nick Bevin

163

1

2

3

KELLY RESIDENCE

JOHN MAINWARING & ASSOCIATES

Situated on a long, thin site at **Casuarina Beach**, the house consists of four distinct components. The 'H' plan was fattened and turned sideways. The ocean-facing double-storey verandah pavilion is separated from a 'fibro sleeping box' by a translucent box that contains the entry, vertical circulation and access to the various spaces within the house. The translucent, polycarbonate wafer filling also provides natural light to the basically introverted, darker sleeping pod on one side and living spaces on the other. The fibro sleeping box is not only a reference frame to the simple and humble historical beach house, but also separates the living pod from the afternoon heat load and street privacy problems. The fourth component is a carport that faces the street. • The main focus of space in this house is on outdoor living. Both levels of the verandah pavilion provide large outdoor areas protected from the blustering weather from the southeast. Indoor spaces have been minimised with the intention of opening out onto external areas. The option to close up the house to protect from northerly winds provides flexibility for internal living when necessary. • The building has simple cross-circulation patterns intersecting on one longitudinal circulation spine. The sleeping box contains four bedrooms; two on the north side have views through to the east via the grand verandah and its undercroft. In between the banks of bedrooms is a shared bathroom on the top level, and a laundry below. The verandah structure contains the kitchen, indoor/outdoor living/dining upstairs, with powder room, rumpus and outdoor spaces under the verandah on the lower level. The bathroom on this level is shared by downstairs bedrooms and beach goers. The verandah structure is reminiscent of the bionic forms of fish bones, as all the rafters and beams are expressed.

4

5

1 Early morning showing carport pavilion, bedroom box and living pavilion separated by polycarbonate wafer
2 View from lantern space to upstairs living
3 East view facing casuarina forest and Pacific Ocean
4 Upstairs external living space
5 Upstairs internal living space
Photography: Bart Maiorana (2,4,5); John Mainwaring (1,3)

1

2

3

KEOGH HOUSE

d.LINEATE architecture + interior design

The Keogh residence, in **suburban Adelaide**, is a significant family home designed to accommodate numerous, diverse activities at one time. It is possible to enter the private section of the home and even use the wonderful steam room/bathhouse while a client or staff from the owner's city office are consulting in the upper studio or having coffee in the café bar. • The residence is loosely zoned into four areas: the foyer and garage are positioned where the original house once stood and still contain the remnants of the old fireplace, a sentimental memory of the original home. The fireplace also acts as an abstract sculpture and folly punctuating the foyer. A diagonal staircase intersects the foyer and transports one to the upper studio/entertainment areas, which double as a magnificent home office and training environment if required. • Open living, café bar and dining spaces are placed at the core of the building with bifold glass doors opening complete walls to the garden and pool. The café bar is pivotal in the open space and suited for coffees or cocktails. It remains uncluttered by typical kitchen mess thanks to the galley pantry within the curved wall and the adjacent stainless steel utility room. This conceals washing areas, food preparation, waste disposal and additional cooking appliances including a steam oven. It is perfect for caterers and leads directly outside for deliveries, recycling and rubbish. • The main building and private living quarters frame the 25-metre lap pool, boardwalk and gardens. A bathhouse, steam room and spa support the clients' healthy lifestyle. • Natural materials, light, ventilation and correct orientation create a relaxed living environment. The principal materials are rammed earth, Kanmantoo stone, steel, glass and Mintaro slate. Jarrah floors and painted ceilings in pear, quince and citrus colours complement the rammed earth and infuse the house with an energetic palette of materials and colours.

1	Porch	18	Services
2	Foyer	19	Shed
3	Garage	20	Bathroom
4	Cloak room	21	Bedroom 3
5	Powder room	22	Steam room
6	Utility	23	Spa
7	Pantry	24	Bathhouse
8	Café bar	25	Deck and boardwalk
9	Living/dining	26	Pool
10	Living 2	27	Studio
11	Conservatory office	28	WC
12	Courtyard	29	Shower
13	Bedroom 1	30	Entertainment room
14	Ensuite	31	Landing
15	Walk-in robe	32	Void
16	Laundry	33	Balcony
17	Bedroom 2		

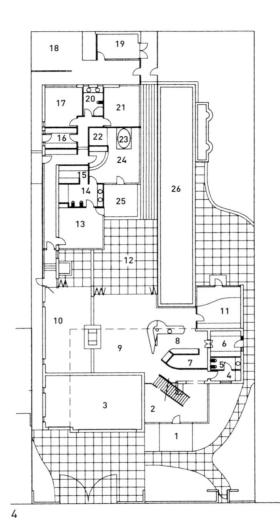

4

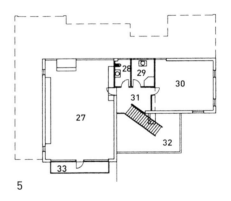

5

1   View from street
2   Exterior at dusk
3   View across lap pool to bath house and bedrooms
4   Ground floor plan
5   First floor plan
6   External courtyard, water feature with bridge

6

9

11

12

10

7   Lounge area with view to bridge corridor
8   Café bar with adjacent steel utility room
9   Evening view of lap pool
10 Bathhouse with steam room, spa and adjacent exercise area
11 Conservatory office with lap pool
12 Bathroom

Photography: Sarah Long Photography

KEW HOUSE

JACKSON CLEMENTS BURROWS ARCHITECTS

The Kew House is located on an existing subdivided tennis court cut into a steep site in **Melbourne's inner east**. The brief called for the car access, master bedroom and living areas to be located on the same level. • The brief provided an opportunity to design a building that immersed itself into its context, not as a stand-alone inanimate object, but as a building that contributed to and formed part of the surrounding ambience. If the ground plane (existing tennis court) was an artificial scar on the landscape, could the new building effect a new condition that repaired, rejuvenated and reconnected with what once was? Could a built solution contribute to the ambience of an existing location by intensifying its intangible ephemeral qualities? How do you make a building that shifts the focal point from architecture to the atmosphere it produces? These questions informed the built solution, the selection of materials, the articulation of interior volumes and the resolution of the architectural form itself. • The first-floor living platform, suspended amongst a canopy of trees and supported by a steel column system, recalls the new growth of self-seeded saplings. The two-tone cladding of the architectural form evokes the colours of the once-dominant indigenous river red gums and the satin finish of the Colorbond contrasts with the dull matte of oxidising zinc. These materials accentuate the liveliness of the constant changes in the light. • The house responds to all orientations in a specific way. Every room in the house orients itself north to maximise a view corridor across the Yarra Bend golf course and the northern suburbs of Melbourne. The west and east openings are kept to a minimum, reducing heat gain and overlooking to neighbouring properties and protecting the occupants from the impact of future development on both east and west boundaries. • In summary, this is a house that merges with the landscape – a response that references, heals, regenerates and strengthens both the physical and atmospheric qualities of its site and surrounds.

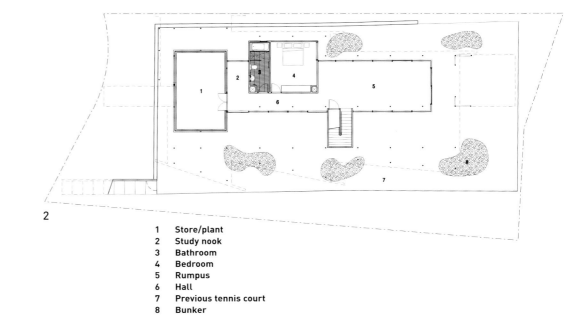

2

1	Store/plant
2	Study nook
3	Bathroom
4	Bedroom
5	Rumpus
6	Hall
7	Previous tennis court
8	Bunker

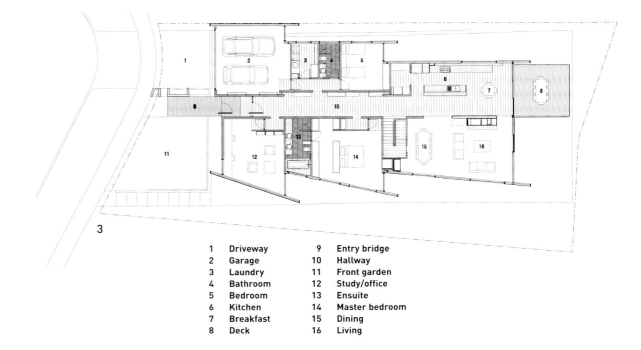

3

1	Driveway	9	Entry bridge
2	Garage	10	Hallway
3	Laundry	11	Front garden
4	Bathroom	12	Study/office
5	Bedroom	13	Ensuite
6	Kitchen	14	Master bedroom
7	Breakfast	15	Dining
8	Deck	16	Living

1   Upper floor and living areas elevated amongst the surrounding landscape
2   Upper level floor plan
3   Lower level floor plan

4

5

6

4   Extended eaves and walls provide solar protection and privacy
5   Living space and kitchen are both divided and connected by the circulation spine and breezeway
6   West elevation
7   Living space becomes a viewing platform
8   Streetscape elevation and entry
9   Children's play area

Photography: John Gollings, Gollings Photography Pty Ltd

1

1 North loggia with lake beyond
2 West façade overlooking lake
3 Concept sketch

LAKE HOUSE

HULENA ARCHITECTS LTD

The owners of this 1970s builder-designed colonial home in **Taupo, New Zealand** wanted it transformed into a lake home with a lodge-like feel. Situated high on a cliff with extensive views of Lake Taupo, the house needed to cater for the extremes of weather experienced throughout the year. Other requirements were for it to be welcoming and comfortable, with facilities for the easy accommodation of overnight guests. • Materials played a key role in the transformation, with the inclusion of cedar rafters and copper roofing, combined with riverstone cladding and black-stained board-and-batten cladding. This layering of complementary textures and elements has lent a two-dimensional building a much-needed third dimension. • Inside, the large living areas have been opened up so that they flow into each other. They extend naturally from the large, outdoor fireplace under the eaves of the outdoor room, through the kitchen, living and family spaces, to the cosy winter snug with its large fireplace. The fine existing billiards room was retained, while the guest bedroom and library have become the master bedroom, so that the owners can enjoy some degree of separation from the other bedrooms upstairs.

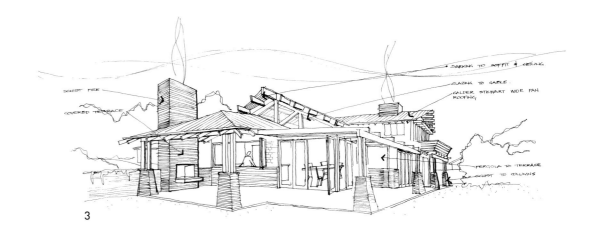

3

2

4

6

7

4   View through dining and kitchen to loggia and exterior fireplace
5   Dining and kitchen
6   Loggia and exterior fireplace
7   Living room

Photography: Simon Devitt

5

1

LANTERN HOUSE

DEM (AUST) PTY LTD

The concept behind this 450-square-metre home on the waterfront at **Cronulla** is the idea of layered translucency. Glass is the main medium – used traditionally for vision, sandblasted for screening, coloured for light enhancement, strengthened for stairs and bridges and used as a substrate for finely sliced marble sheets to create a translucent privacy façade to the public street elevation. This spider-marble and glass veneer filters sunlight in the morning to the main bedroom suite and at night glows like a Chinese onyx lantern. • The circulation spine and stairs on the northern boundary are all in glass. Additional sandblasted external glass screens and extensive external louvres allow light deep into the home, while providing privacy and climatic control. A pond, water feature and the raised pool extend the northern spine out to the bay. • Bright accent coloured glass is used on the western elevation: reds, yellows and oranges complement the muted tone of the other house materials: grey steel, limestone, timber, zinc and aluminium. • Where the house is cut into the ridge, the exposed sandstone is left, revealed as a natural backdrop. The excavated stone is reused in rough chiselled form for retaining walls and external accent – contrasting in both colour and texture with the smooth and fine glass and metal in the building. • Glass-wrapped light wells are dropped into the depth of the building to illuminate and ventilate the internal rooms. The open plan and glass internal walls allow the living spaces a series of filtered views back towards the water while allowing the owners to retreat to relative enclosure when required. The double-storey family room and kitchen on the ground floor spill out onto the rear deck. The middle level contains the children's and guest bedrooms, entry and garage. The top level is a contained parent's retreat with bedroom, bathroom, study, gym and changing room extending onto a large roof terrace.

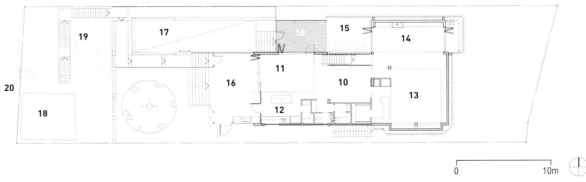

1   Street elevation at dusk, with glowing translucent marble/starfire glass panels
2   Upper level floor plan
3   Middle level floor plan
4   Ground level floor plan

1	Garage	9	Deck	17	Pool
2	Entry	10	Dining	18	Boat shed
3	Lightwell	11	Family	19	Sandstone bluff
4	Guest room	12	Kitchen	20	Gunamatta Bay
5	Bedroom	13	Games	21	Robe
6	Glass bridge	14	Living	22	Gym
7	Void over family room	15	Lightwell/courtyard	23	Study
8	Children's play area	16	Verandah	24	Roof

5

6

7

8

5　Evening view of street garden elevation
6　Family area opens onto decks and pool
7　Glass stairwell
8　Double-volume family and dining space with glass
　　bridge and stairs
9　Bayside elevation at dusk with coloured glass panels
　　and house reflected in lap pool

**Photography: Kata Bayer (1,7,9);
Marian Riabic (5,6,8)**

9

1

2   3   4

1   The original pool and backyard was transformed into a more functional and accessible space
2   Night view of main living space
3   Internal living spaces flow directly into outdoor entertaining
4   Centrally located kitchen services both front and back living areas
5   Outdoor deck and renovated pool area cater for regular entertaining with ease
6   Ground floor plan
7   Symmetrically designed, the master ensuite makes the most of a small space
Photography: Nik West (1,4,5,7); Mark Cranitch (2,3)

5

LIDO RESIDENCE

BAYDEN GODDARD DESIGN

The client purchased this **Queensland waterfront** property, originally a 1960's brick veneer residence, without an internal inspection. The dilapidated residence revealed dark and damp interior spaces that were very restrictive and required extensive renovation. • The client brief for the residence was to create a single-storey home suited to raising a young family with the flexibility to accommodate their changing requirements. • The pitched roof and ceiling in the main space, combined with high sloped glass, maximise the available northern light, creating a vibrant interior. The use of timber flooring adds further warmth to the living spaces. The main living space is designed to be the central hub of the house, allowing supervision of the children in all areas of the property. The location of windows became critical to balancing supervision, views and privacy. Maximum privacy was required for the living space so the design of the windows directs views above and below the neighbouring house. While the central hallway allows visual access for supervision throughout the property, it also provides cross-ventilation. Combined with secure sliding screens, the house becomes a 'breezeway'. • Externally, the design was also influenced by maintaining the existing pool, courtyard and jetty locations to take advantage of setbacks while also controlling the project cost. By refurbishing the existing waterfront courtyard, the residence remains on one child-friendly level. The dominant views to the waterfront are controlled through the use of glass and solid balustrades, creating a private entertaining area. The front courtyard/play area is connected to the children's rumpus room and takes advantage of the carport as a multipurpose play area. By experimenting with lightweight FC products, colours and horizontal forms, this single-storey residence provides a contemporary feel to an established suburb.

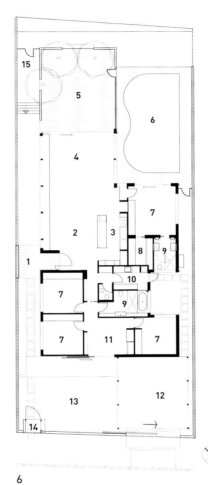

1	Entry
2	Dining
3	Kitchen
4	Living
5	Deck
6	Pool
7	Bedroom
8	Walk-in robe
9	Bathroom
10	Laundry
11	Rumpus
12	Carport
13	Outdoor play area
14	Gatehouse
15	Access to jetty

6

7

LILYFIELD HOUSE

PETER TONKIN AND ELLEN WOOLLEY WITH TONKIN ZULAIKHA GREER

The house for two architects on a small and difficult site became a laboratory for experiment and investigation. • The site, in **Sydney's inner west**, is of strong character. The western part, falling more than 6 metres across the frontage, contains major natural rock outcrops and floating boulders, and adjoins a reserve full of eucalypts, both significant remnants of the indigenous landscape. The eastern part of the site is at street level, and its surrounds are more aggressive and urban. To the east are good views of Sydney and the harbour. • The accommodation is simple: three bedrooms upstairs, on the main level a library and a big room containing living, kitchen and dining opening onto a terrace, and at street level, a workroom, laundry and garage. The big room focuses in three directions: east to the city skyline and the terrace, west to the theatrical central 'fire' – the kitchen with its white altar for cooking – and north to a secluded grotto hollowed out of the boulders, a tiny back yard. • The house's southern circulation zone, in concrete and brick, buffers a busy road and washes the house with daylight. A 'carpet' of timber: bridge, stairs, balcony and furniture, extends through this zone, bridging between its massive walls. The northern light of the clerestory floods this long, tall slot. The street wall is a plane cut away for openings, its exterior in two shades of black. The central wall plays off solid with void. Thick sculpted piers bear three storeys of uniting concrete beams. The piers hold carefully crafted light niches as well as storage, timber cabinets and services. • Inside the simple northern box that houses the living spaces, rooms are calmly proportioned rectangles, maximum accommodation in a tight area, in contrast to the vertical drama of the circulation buffer.

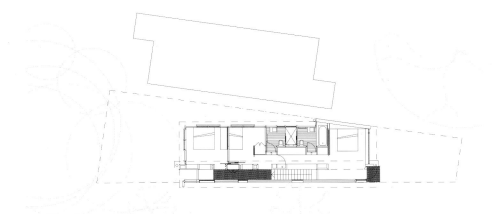

2

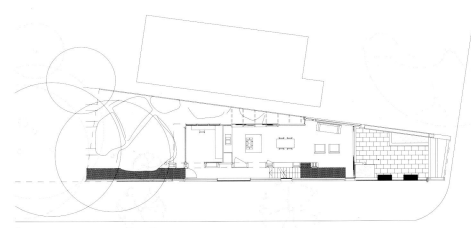

3

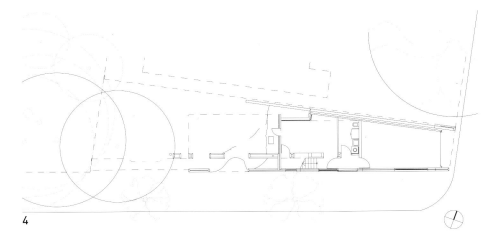

Opposite:
    West elevation floats over the retained sandstone boulders on the site

2   First floor plan

3   Ground floor plan

4   Lower ground floor plan

4

5

6

7

8

9

5   East elevation opens to the elevated terrace
6   The north-facing clerestory floods the house with light
7   Exterior with black three-storey street wall
8   View from kitchen through living to terrace
9   A thickened storage wall separates the stairwell

**Photography: Patrick Bingham-Hall (p184,6,7);
Richard Glover (5,8,9)**

1

2

3

4

5

6

MELI HOUSE

CORBEN ARCHITECTS
INTERIORS BY DECOROOM

The Meli House is a new four-bedroom residence located on a small southeast-facing site in the **Sydney suburb of Mosman** with panoramic views over Balmoral Beach towards Middle Head. • The house was designed and built in close collaboration with the owners, interior designer Ruth Meli and builder Joe Meli. • The brief called for a contemporary styled house with a well planned interior that maximized the view and aspect from each room. • The residence is designed over three levels with the garage, gymnasium and store on the lower floor. The middle floor comprises two separate living areas divided by the entry and central circulation space with its stunning stone-faced spine wall and 'floating' timber stair. The upper level contains four bedrooms and associated bathrooms. • The house was designed to be deliberately understated to provide a backdrop for a limited but rich palette of beautiful finishes selected by the owners including limestone and timber parquetry floors and extensive timber veneered joinery. • Combined with a range of modern comfortable furniture and artwork, the house is an excellent showpiece for the owners and their architects.

8

1   Level three floor plan
2   Level two floor plan
3   Level one floor plan
4&8 Street façade
5   Grand entry hall with stairs connecting the three levels
6   Flow-through casual living area linking rear garden to front entertaining terrace
7   Kitchen is integrated with family room
9   Ensuite bathroom
Photography: Craig Bryant

7

9

1

2

3

MILSONS POINT APARTMENT

STANIC HARDING PTY LTD

The client brief was to transform a poorly planned apartment in a former multi-storey office building in **Milsons Point**. The existing condition denied the occupants connections to views and light by stacking bedrooms along most of the perimeter. The kitchen was also effectively disconnected from the dining area and the narrow living space by being tucked into the rear of the apartment. • The architects' response was to strip the apartment back to its bare shell, allowing major replanning to encompass the new requirements of a considered entry sequence, connection to sky, light and view and the separation of public and private spaces. • One of the three bedrooms was relocated into the back of the apartment, allowing the two remaining bedrooms to be increased in size with better connections to light and the view. The public spaces then increased in size along the perimeter window. The third bedroom became a guest/study space raised above the main floor level. • The kitchen/dining space was brought into the main living/entry zone. The main wall was clad in full-height mirror panels that at once doubled the perception of available space and reflected the harbour view into the body of the apartment. A chocolate timber floor defined the main spaces, with very plush shag-pile carpet defining the lounge and bedroom spaces. • Joinery played an important role in this transformation. The main kitchen joinery is a rectangular pod that divides the kitchen and study/guest room. It houses the main kitchen bench and associated storage on one side, general storage at each end and the study on the other side. A dark timber veneer wall unit forms the edge of the living space and presents as a series of solid engaged columns that house audiovisual and entertainment equipment. A sliding screen that forms part of the unit's composition when closed hides the plasma screen.

1   Detail of main kitchen bench looking to day bed
2   Mirrored wall reflects view and increases the sense of space
3   Lounge area defined by carpet island
4   Floor plan
5   Main bedroom entry showing airconditioning grille detail and part of secondary robe space

6

7

8

9

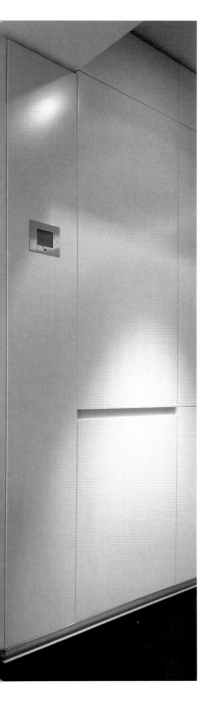

10

6   View of kitchen unit complete with built-in dining table
7   Ensuite bathroom showing custom Corian vanity floating in front of mirror
8   View into main bedroom and guest bathroom showing translucent glass screen
9   Joinery pod detail at study/guest room entry
10   Mirror used to extend space in main bedroom
      Photography: Paul Gosney

1

3

2

4

MODICA RESIDENCE

JOHN MAINWARING & ASSOCIATES

This house, at **Queensland's Sunshine Beach**, is a Pacific Rim hybrid designed for a Toyko-based American academic and his Japanese wife. The challenge was to abstract aspects of the traditional fibro holiday house and Japanese influences, keeping to a strict budget. The slightly angled roofs and fibro walls evoke the traditional holiday home, while the opal and clear polycarbonate walls, together with the Japanese tatami room and bathhouse echo modern Japanese styles. • A double-height lantern entry with vertical circulation provides access to double-storey living areas on the west side of the 'catamaran' plan, with bridge access to the 'outrigger' sleeping pod to the east. The bedroom and living spaces are separated. The living wing contains an exotic bathhouse that is used to service this area of the house. As a third bedroom may only be required at certain times during the year, the combined study/living room/third bedroom allows for flexibility in use. In the main living area, a large retractable door provides for indoor/outdoor living, capitalising on ocean glimpses and views of the dunal valley. • The house is situated in a long, thin, heavily vegetated dunal valley surrounded by other properties on a site that is landlocked and introverted. It is a simple lightweight structure coloured to complement the surrounding flora, and shows empathy for its natural location, in contrast to many neighbouring 'heavy monsters' that dominate the landscape. The flat roof floats on top of the schlerophyll flora and fauna ecosystem, merging the articulated tectonics and the dynamics of the natural environment.

1 H-plan with atrium main wing and 'outrigger' wing
2 Elevation showing living wing and sleeping wing
3 Fibro, steel and timber construction
4 Retractable glazing to living and dining spaces
5 Internal view of stairwell heat chimney lantern

Photography: John Mainwaring

5

MOONAH LINKS HOUSE

JACKSON CLEMENTS BURROWS ARCHITECTS

This building evolved from a highly considered landscape response. Located high on the crest of a coastal dunescape, the Moonah Links House is challenged by the importance of sensitively placing new buildings in a significant coastal environment. Overlooking the Moonah Links golf course on **Victoria's Mornington Peninsula**, the form carefully hugs the steep topography and protects this four-bedroom, split-level retreat residence from the extreme weather to which the site is exposed. • From the outset the approach was to design a house that would be visually camouflaged and modest in appearance. Two devices were used: the first was to develop a cost-effective form, which in silhouette would mimic the surrounding hills. The form also resulted in split-level internal spaces that allowed effective space planning, taking into account briefing constraints relating to separation. Critical to the brief was the ability to accommodate guests in a separate and private zone while still providing the opportunity for the clients' adult children to stay as well. • The second strategy was to select external materials that would blend with the surrounding colours and texture of the immediate landscape. Varying tones of seasonal colour are expressed in the vertical bands of Colorbond cladding, providing a subtle reference to the long shadows that are cast across the undulations in the dunescape at dawn and dusk. This device sets up a dialogue between the building and the landscape itself, which assists in the expression of concealment – a modest shelter, connected with the landscape and camouflaged from view.

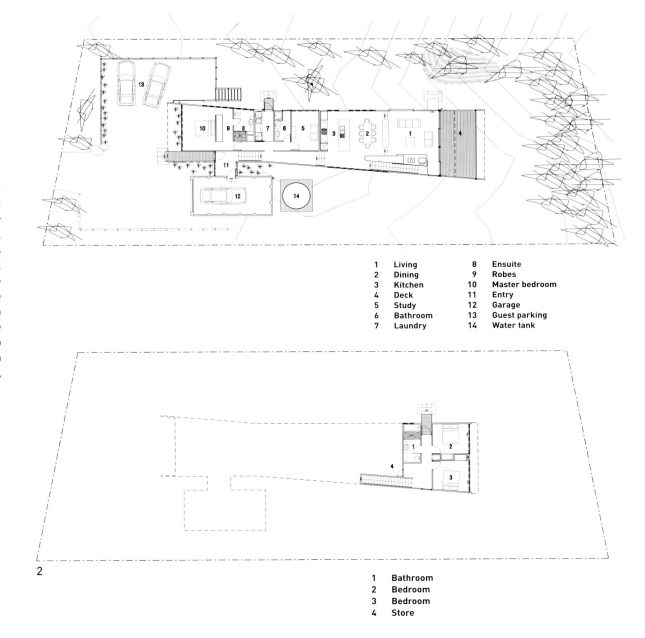

1	Living	8	Ensuite
2	Dining	9	Robes
3	Kitchen	10	Master bedroom
4	Deck	11	Entry
5	Study	12	Garage
6	Bathroom	13	Guest parking
7	Laundry	14	Water tank

1	Bathroom
2	Bedroom
3	Bedroom
4	Store

Opposite:

East elevation with protected deck

2   Upper and lower level floor plans

3

4

3   Main living space
4   North elevation with immediate relationship to landscape
5   Eaves overhang for western solar protection
6   Banded Colorbond cladding for camouflage
7   Elevated deck with golf course views
8   Section
9   Form responds to topography

Photography: Shannon McGrath

5

6

7

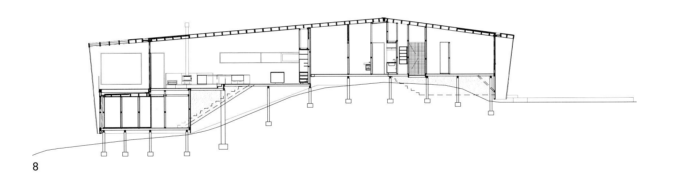

8

9

199

1

2

1   Living room with view back to older part of residence
2   Addition manipulates site levels to form a carport under the house
3   Zincalume (metal) box articulates existing and new parts of the residence
4   Floor plan

MT HAWTHORN RESIDENCE

IREDALE PEDERSEN HOOK ARCHITECTS

The residence is located on a long, thin, gently sloping corner block in the inner-city suburb of **Mount Hawthorn, Perth**. The existing 1940's brick and tile residence was complete with a 'tacked on' lean-to addition to the rear. The primary frontage of the house was well cared for, so the focus of attention was to the neglected rear of the block. • Both client and architect had a desire for the addition to be new and modern in appearance without making it so different that it didn't read as part of a single residence. The solution was for the main part of the addition to reverse the material palette of the existing house. The dominant reddish brown of the bricks highlighted with white mortar of the old becomes predominantly white render with a number of 'clipped on' reddish-brown elements in the new addition. These two complementary parts are then visually broken by a cantilevering zincalume 'box', forming the dining space beyond. • The addition uses the site's slope to step and delineate the interconnected spaces while the structure provides an openness that mediates between the individual roomed nature of the house and more contemporary open-plan living. The clients love to cook and entertain so the kitchen was placed at the transition point between the old and new, making it central to the house. As the addition 'snakes' its way across the site, it provides a clear spatial connection with the old house, achieves north orientation to the main living space, and uses the sloping site to good effect with the master bedroom and ensuite 'leaping' over the top of the new carport. Along the diagonal journey through the addition, views of the park are carefully framed with the bedroom being high enough to see over the surrounding area to the horizon beyond.

3

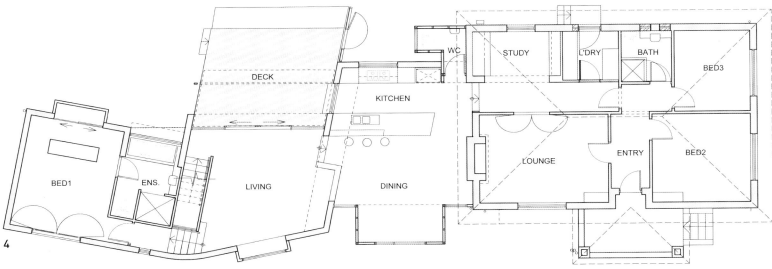

4

5

5   Rear garden
6   Living space with bedroom stair
7   Curved wall with built-in sofa seat
8   Exterior detail of surface articulation and
     cantilevers
9   View across kitchen/dining space to living
     space with subtle variation of levels

**Photography: Robert Frith,
Acorn Photo Agency (1,3,5–9);
courtesy Iredale Pedersen Hook
Architects (2)**

6

7

8

9

1

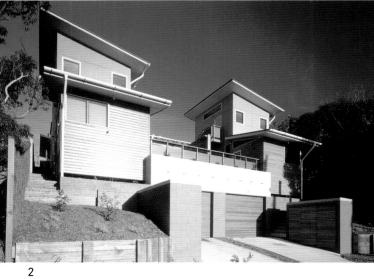

2

3

4

NELLIES

BOURNE + BLUE ARCHITECTURE

Conceived as exquisite pavilions on the top of a sand dune, these two houses at the south end of **Boomerang beach** on the New South Wales north coast offer some unique accommodation. • The various spaces of the houses are separated by decks and outdoor space, allowing vegetation to come between the buildings, blurring inside and outside. The pavilions are highly crafted timber boxes, providing a tactile and human scale. The proportions of the spaces alter depending on use: a soaring ceiling for the living spaces, a low curving plywood ceiling to provide intimacy for the dining space. A spatially dynamic bunkroom provides delight for children of all ages. • There are several ways to bathe here: fully outdoor on returning from the beach, a bath partially outdoors with privacy, or an open bath in the 'turret' bedroom. There are several ways to live here, too: on top of the dune, with built-in seats and screens, or shielded from the elements with the living room closed up, or in the protected court, away from the breezes. The climate dictates how the various spaces are used. • The brief was to design two compact houses, side-by-side. The clients are two couples, who intended to use one of the homes as an investment (holiday rental) property and the other for their own use. The other priority was that each of the dwellings be designed to thoughtfully accommodate two families. The two homes have a mirrored layout. A central spine connecting the two dwellings contains utility spaces such as bathrooms, surfboard rooms and kitchens. Each dwelling has a two-storey structure at the rear of the site containing bedrooms and a separate turret bedroom overlooking the beach.

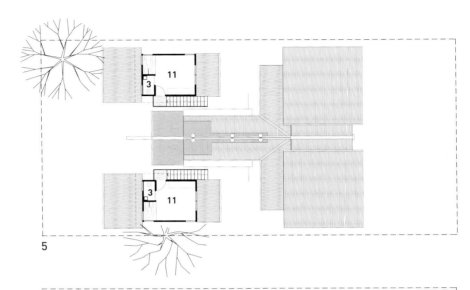

5

1	Cars
2	Storage
3	Bathroom
4	Bedroom 1
5	Ensuite
6	Bunkroom
7	Outdoor bathroom
8	Laundry
9	Kitchen
10	Living/dining
11	Bedroom 2

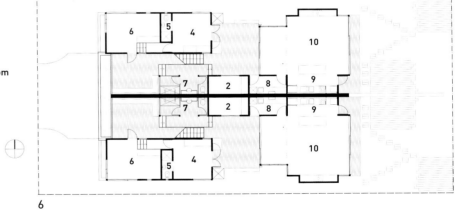

6

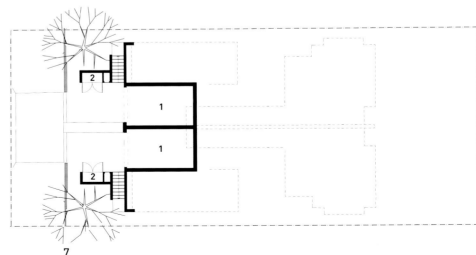

7

1	Turret bedroom
2	View from street
3	Western deck
4	View from beach
5	Level three floor plan
6	Level two floor plan
7	Level one floor plan

8

9

10

Photography: Brett Boardman

12

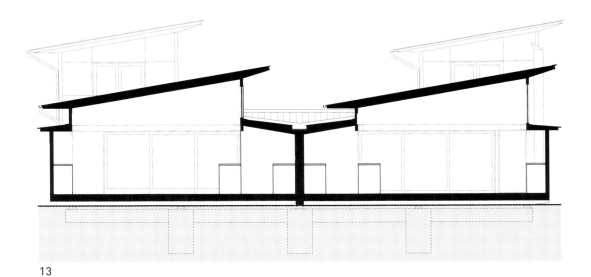

13

11

1

1   Eastern courtyard and pool with view through house to ocean
2   West elevation showing massive pleated off-form concrete wall
3   Upper floor plan
4   Lower floor plan

WRIGHT FELDHUSEN ARCHITECTS

The site is elevated and faces west with spectacular views of the **Indian Ocean**. Typically, with the west coast, the summer afternoon enjoyment of this magnificent location can be reduced by the hot setting sun and the often blustery southwesterly sea breeze. The main external living areas and swimming pool are located on the east side of the residence, which is protected from the harsh afternoon sun and wind. Because of the site's slope, the upper-level living areas are at ground level to the eastern side and above the lower level base to the western side, making the house appear as two levels from the street (west) and single-level at the rear (east).
• The main living level of the house is articulated as a glass pavilion with the roof hovering above. Up-lights and high-level windows enable the roof to float and almost peel away. The roof follows the line of the site's slope, which is also along the line of maximum height as defined by the local council. The articulation of the architecture enables the eastern external living area to have a protected visual connection to the ocean, through the glass. The slope of the roof, angling down to the western horizon has the added advantage of closing the aperture to direct afternoon sun penetration. • The lower level areas are a more solid 'base' to the upper living pavilion and house the children's bedrooms and play areas. • The front western elevation is dominated by a massive off-form white concrete wall. The thickness and intrinsic mass of this element reinforce the sense of barrier and protection from the sometimes hostile ocean side weather. • The inspiration for the different textures and tones of the building materials comes from the client's fashion background, and is reflected in the 'pleated' pattern on the concrete. This theme is carried through to the fireplace inside where the articulation of the concrete is contrasted by a series of horizontal CaesarStone blade shelves and alcoves. The kitchen has no splash-back wall and is surrounded by sliding glass that acts as a servery and reinforces the visual connection with all living areas (outside and in). The kitchen bench continues outside to form a bench on the other side of the window.

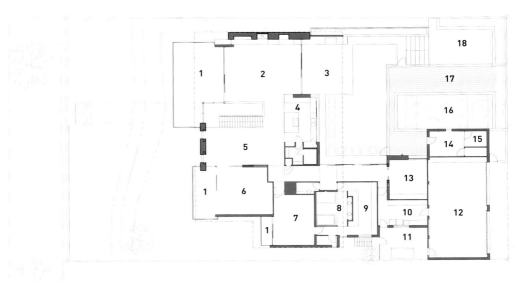

3

1	Balcony	8	Ensuite	15	Sauna	22	Sewing room
2	Lounge	9	Walk-in robe	16	Pool	23	Entry
3	Terrace	10	Laundry	17	Deck	24	Vestibule
4	Kitchen	11	Drying court	18	Lawn terrace	25	Bath
5	Dining	12	Garage	19	Store	26	Robe
6	Library	13	Study	20	Playroom	27	Bedroom
7	Bedroom	14	Gym	21	Video room	28	Cellar

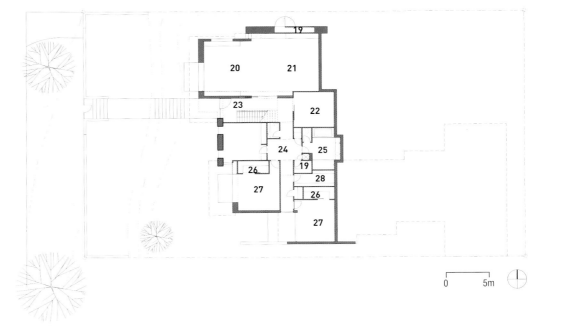

4

0   5m

2

5

6

7

5   Night view of kitchen and terrace
6   View from kitchen through to lounge
7   View of kitchen from dining
Photography: Jon Chisholm

OCEAN HOUSE

WOLVERIDGE ARCHITECTS

The brief for this project had two main criteria: first, the physical accommodation requirements and second, that the building be sensitively sited and not obtrusive from any aspect of its exposed surroundings. • The **Cape Schanck** site comprises a dramatic ridgeline overlooking the fairways of two golf courses and Bass Strait. The sporadically located protected moonah trees had to be built around and a restrictive building envelope also influenced the location of the building. • The floor plan of the 444-square-metre house is axial and comprises two main sections, each a two-storey construction in itself and linked by a single-storey kitchen element and private courtyard space. Externally, a weathered zinc form identifies this connection. • In order to facilitate the accommodation, around 300 cubic metres of earth were excavated, stockpiled and replaced against the completed building as a manufactured contour – like an extension of the links-type landscape. The incision into the earth's ridgeline enabled the construction of a two-storey structure with one storey emerging above the natural ground line. • The constructed dwelling provides a protected and private north-facing external courtyard, free of the direct elements. The house is effectively built around this external space. The living spaces and kitchen hover around and open up onto the courtyard and capture the western views offered by the site.

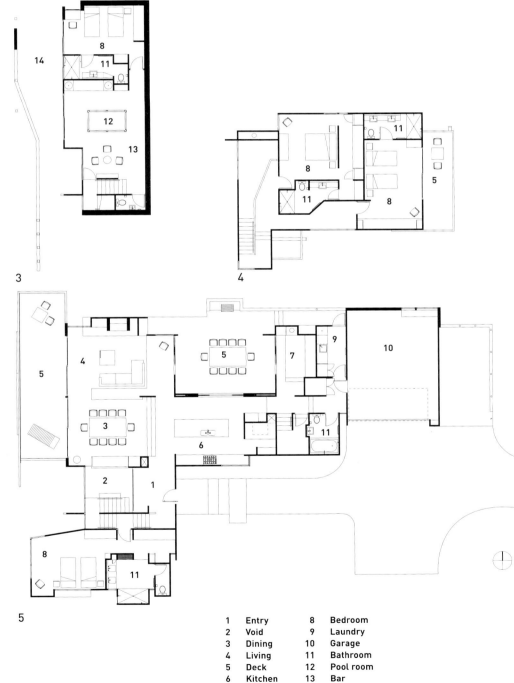

Opposite:

    Excavated entry element
2   House in context of ridgeline and backdrop of moonah trees
3   Lower ground floor plan
4   First floor plan
5   Upper ground floor plan

1	Entry	8	Bedroom
2	Void	9	Laundry
3	Dining	10	Garage
4	Living	11	Bathroom
5	Deck	12	Pool room
6	Kitchen	13	Bar
7	Study	14	Terrace

6

6 Looking up from the rough
7 Living and deck connecting with moonah tree
8 Master bedroom
9 West façade elevation at dusk

Photography: Derek Swalwell Photography

7

8

9

PADDINGTON HOUSE

INDYK ARCHITECTS PTY LTD

First impressions of the old terrace house in **Paddington**, in **inner-city Sydney** were the benign northerly aspect and the hugeness of the borrowed landscape view of nearby Trumper Park. • The clients' brief was about 'living on the site' and making use of the inherent positive aspects. The existing terrace seemed not to realise that it was situated on the edge of the old valley. It had boxed itself away from the north, and turned itself inwards. • The constraint of a 4-metre-wide terrace was to be counterbalanced by the openness of space. The park became the feature foreground and background for living. A refined simple plan was created to extend the limitations and perception of the narrow terrace. Existing cross walls were removed so that each floor became a long north–south room with cross-ventilation from both aspects. • The material palette was limited to off-form concrete floors and ceilings, with steel portal frames to create the new structural diaphragm; recycled jarrah timber was used for all joinery; windows and doors were steel-framed. • The house, like a camera box, opens and closes its aperture to the northern sun. The counterbalanced doors allow 3-metre-wide apertures. The protective aspect of the site supports this openness, summer and winter. • Lighting became an essential design element. The drama of the morning northern light is balanced by the soft southern illumination through opaque glass. Daylight shifts to night with the drama of indirect light reflecting off ceilings and floors, extending the perspective of the rooms. Bathrooms glow a little like lantern boxes, with their illuminated opaque glass cross walls.

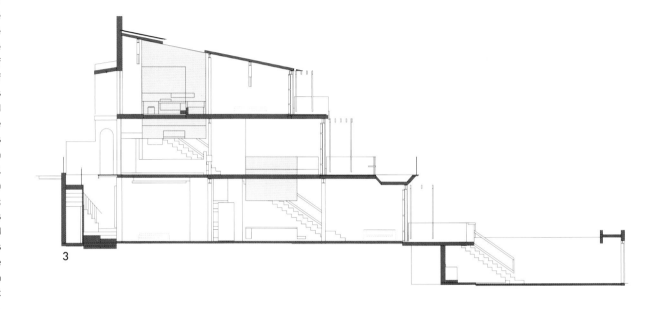

3

1   Entry level kitchen view
2   View of kitchen from under stair
3   Section

2

4

5

6

Photography: Murray Fredericks

7

8

9

PALM BEACH HOUSE

WORKSHOP 1 PTY LTD

The brief was to convert three apartments in two existing buildings into one family house that included a private area for the adults and a space to allow them to work from home. Two fundamental spatial requirements were to activate a private outdoor courtyard room, and to protect the inhabitants from the view of people using the beach. A decision was made early in the project to retain the existing 1950's brick block building mass and work within its spatial framework. This allowed the architects to adapt the house to a sustainable future by engaging the thermal mass and utilising cross-ventilation and heat stack effects to control heat. Underground water storage and natural filtration systems were installed to use collected roof water for laundry, bathroom, garden and drinking needs. • The architecture has been expressed as a series of finely crafted, space-making furniture pieces that have been inserted into and grafted onto the fabric of the existing building. The window boxes in the living room and bedrooms puncture the envelope of the brick skin and create a new seat or table while providing protection from the sun and wind. The windows slide over the external elevation so that they disappear when viewed from the inside. The new sunroom and northwestern wall have been wrapped around the brick mass. The northwestern wall uses a stack effect to passively cool the rest of the house. In the colder months the warm air is stored in the stairwell and then distributed around the house by fans. • All of the new joinery pieces have been made from recycled Australian hardwood (spotted gum) that has been retrieved from old wool stores and industrial buildings. The patina and grain of this beautiful timber gives a special quality to the spaces that were made in and around the house.

2

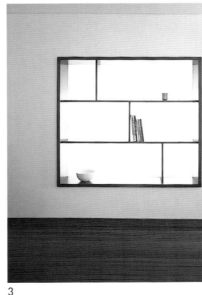

3

4

1   Courtyard elevation showing the kitchen opened up with doors hidden
2   Main bedroom and bathroom are connected by a deck that
     overlooks Pittwater
3   Translucent glass shelving unit allows light from the stairwell
     into the main bedroom
4   Beach elevation showing northwest wall and window boxes

Photography: Kilian O'Sullivan, www.light-room.co.uk

1

1   View upon arrival
2   Master ensuite
3   View of coastline beyond
Following pages:
      View upon entry
Photography: Aperture Photography

THE PANORAMA

PAUL UHLMANN ARCHITECTS

The Panorama house is a collection of sculptural elements united by an axial spine, standing confidently in its rural environment. The textures and details of the building, both internally and externally, explore this sculptural interest at their own scale. The planning of the building creates independent living, sleeping and guest zones that optimise the spectacular panoramic views of the site overlooking **Queensland's Gold Coast**. • The clients required a contemporary and unique building reflective of their personalities. The Panorama sits confidently upon the hillside, in empathy with the environment, having a relatively small and low impact footprint upon the site. • The 392-square-metre home is split into three pavilions, fulfilling the clients' requirements for separate guest and bedroom areas away from public living spaces. These three spaces are united by a passageway and the roof entity. Glass bridgeways connect to private spaces, which can be shut off physically from more public zones, by a series of sliding doors. These separate zones can act together, or independently if required, creating a dwelling with flexibility. • Division of spaces allowed the use of internal sculptural elements, creating interest and warmth within the expansive plan. This sculptural interest was continued externally with an exploration of textures, details and form.

2

3

223

THE PARADISIO

PAUL UHLMANN ARCHITECTS

The Paradisio is located on a hill top overlooking a popular surf beach on **Queensland's Gold Coast**. The 800-square-metre building is sited on the crown of the hill, with balconies cantilevered over a steep drop off. Living areas were elevated to the first level to take advantage of sweeping views to the distant islands, mountain hinterland and the headland to the south. • The ground level is an activities space relating to the 25-metre lap pool that runs parallel to the beach below. This level also contains quiet accommodation and wine cellars. • The building form is made up of a series of flying roofs that are anchored to the ground with a stone-clad base. A large screened area is located above the entry to enclose an elevated drying court and rainwater tanks. • Two elevated decks have been created to provide alternate dining areas, depending on the prevailing winds. The interior of the residence has some robust finishes to cater for the clients' five children. An extensive native landscape has been planted that will provide a concealed entry to the residence in the years to come.

Opposite:
Northern deck and screened entry
2   View from beach
3   Ground floor plan
4   First floor plan
5   Second floor plan

2

3

4

5

1	Entry	7	Games room	13	Balcony
2	Bedroom	8	Garage	14	Sitting room
3	Cellar	9	Driveway	15	Kitchen
4	Bathroom	10	Laundry	16	Living
5	Pool deck	11	Office	17	Study
6	Pool	12	Dining		

6

7

8

9

10

6   Lap pool
7   Approach to house at night
8   Eastern deck
9   Entry stair
10   Sitting area

Photography: Matt Kennedy

1   North side from beach
2   Living room pergola and deck
3   View from beach
4   Lookout
5   View from entry through to beach
6   Main level floor plan

1

2

3

PARAPARAUMU HOUSE

PARSONSON ARCHITECTS

This is a beach house for a family of five, located on the **Kapiti Coast**, north of **Wellington**. The intention was for the house to create a story of passage, from suburbia to the beach and the horizon beyond. • From the street, the house appears as a slightly ad hoc arrangement of separated forms, with hardiflex boxes anchored to the ground and lighter forms floating around the side, leading through to the beach. • The living area is a raised pavilion from which to enjoy the hot summers and views of the sea. • Metaphors related to the location are threaded through the design, some are literal and some very abstract. These are present as one passes through or stays in the house, adding a resonance that is not necessarily fully discovered. • The house is close to the beach and exposed to the prevailing northwesterly winds. A pallete of non-corrosive materials have been used and are designed to weather.

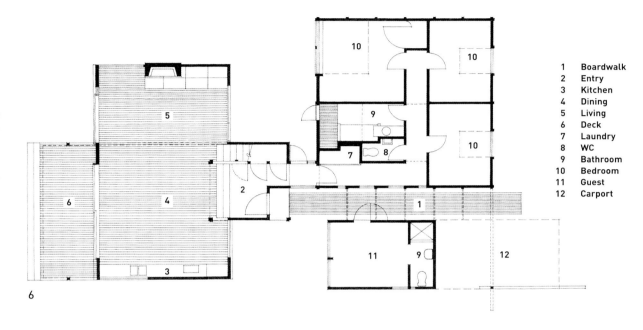

1	Boardwalk
2	Entry
3	Kitchen
4	Dining
5	Living
6	Deck
7	Laundry
8	WC
9	Bathroom
10	Bedroom
11	Guest
12	Carport

6

4

5

7

8

9

10

7   Kitchen and dining
8   Boardwalk to front door
9   Living room
10 Bedroom bunks

Photography: Paul McCredie

PEKAPEKA HOUSE

PARSONSON ARCHITECTS

The house is located at **Pekapeka Beach**, a small seaside settlement one hour's drive north of **Wellington**. It is a small one-bedroom house for a working couple who work in Wellington and Palmerston North. • The house is set on gently undulating dune lands, facing northwest, looking across the road and lower dunes out to the Tasman Sea and Kapiti Island to the west. • It is intended that the house both relate to the horizontality of this landscape and also be at odds with it, as if it had been left there, or washed up. • The exterior is composed of a rhythm of painted fibre cement panels. Elements of wall, roof beam, roof layers and brise soleil are expressed separately, with light entering in places in between. There is a sense of horizontal and vertical layering, and metaphorically a sense of dislocation or decomposition of parts, as if a creature or construction had been left high and dry above the tide.

Opposite:
    North end
2   Floor plan
3   View from road

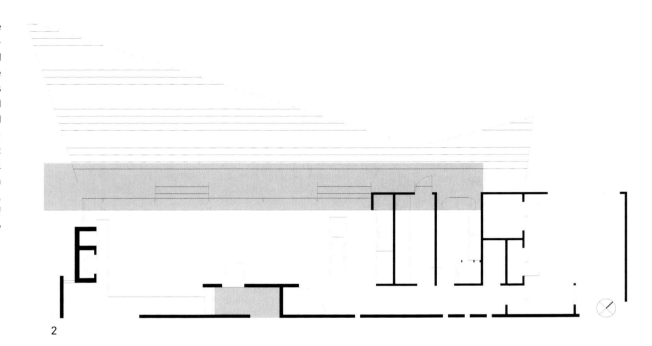

2

3

4   Dining
5&8   Entry
6   Deck
7   Bathroom
9   Kitchen
10   Living room

Photography: Paul McCredie

7

8

9

10

1

2

3

1   West elevation: first impression from driveway is of unconventional sculpture in suburbia
2   Skylight above stairwell emphasises unconventional wall angles
3   Northeast corner
4   Exterior entry has angled walls and stepped volumes around the giant pivot entry door
5   First floor plan
6   Ground floor plan

POINT CHEVALIER HOUSE

ANDREW LISTER ARCHITECT

This house, in **Point Chevalier, Auckland**, is located on a small (323-square-metre) site, a rear subdivided lot with neighbouring houses built on the site boundaries. • The brief was to create a new three-bedroom first home for two architecture-loving accountants, keeping to a modest budget. The couple requested a piece of Japanese sculpture/architecture set into their very suburban landscape. Because of the site size and lack of views, the design brief was for a more inward-looking house, as if there were no other adjacent houses. • The 162-square-metre house is designed in two volumes, each identified by its own cladding, both paying homage to the New Zealand building tradition and Kiwi aesthetic. • A single-storey white volume surrounds a double-storey black cube volume. The white volume is clad in painted compressed sheet cladding, the black cube in a random-thickness stained timber panelling. Both are traditional New Zealand bach cladding materials revitalised with modern Japanese sculptural aesthetics. The change in levels was dictated by strict council development controls. • The theme of volumes continues within the house. Spaces are variable, with sliding screens offering the potential to break rooms at will or to utilise a larger living/dining space when preferred. The double-height dining space meant stretching the budget and squeezing the rooms, but achieves an extraordinary feeling of lightness and space in such a small house.

4

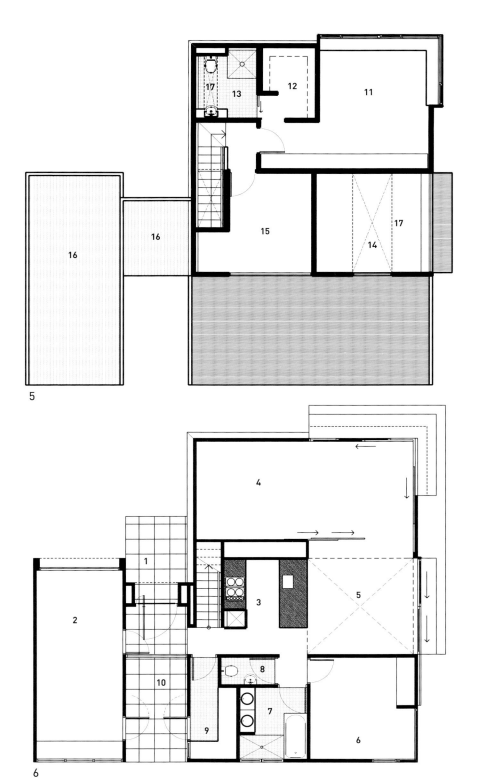

5

6

1   Entry
2   Garage
3   Kitchen
4   Living
5   Dining
6   Bedroom
7   Bathroom
8   WC
9   Laundry
10 Service yard
11 Bedroom
12 Change room
13 Ensuite
14 Void
15 Office
16 Roof
17 Skylight over

7

8

7   Floating bathroom cabinetry and subtle textural materials
8   Interior void embodies sculptural approach to space, material and styles
9   Interior void: sundial skylight slices ceiling while chandeliers redefine the style
10   Kitchen of abstracted timber, mirror and stainless steel
11   Horizontal glazed floating window with screening elements

Photography: Becky Nunes

9

10

11

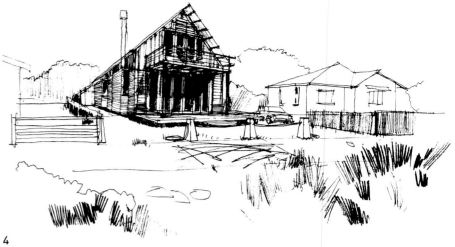

1. Sea view from living area
2. Main bedroom
3. Bedroom balcony balustrade detail
4. Sketch by architect Ric Slessor
5. Bach front bathed in morning sunshine
6. Early morning interior
7. First floor plan
8. Ground floor plan

Photography: Nick Bevin

1

2   3

4

5

POURERERE BACH

BEVIN + SLESSOR ARCHITECTS

This new bach replaces an earlier, self-built, 'low-slung' family bach. The design was conceived as a single and simple gabled form reminiscent of the hull of an upturned fishing boat. This form allowed the floor space and volume to be maximised within the site's planning restrictions. • Living spaces were kept open-plan on the ground floor and were positioned to the east and north to maximise access to outdoors and the sweeping coastal landscape views. Large bi-folding doors allow the extension of the living area onto the deck and allow uninterrupted views to the beach. Timber louvres each side allow for adjustable ventilation in the east wall. • The main bedroom upstairs takes in spectacular views of the coast while a secondary living space doubles as additional sleeping space when required. • The open space behind the bach catches the last sun of the day and provides for barbeques and 'after fishing' activities, protected from the regular summer evening on-shore breezes. • The selection of the exterior palette of materials was based on durability and relative low maintenance in the aggressive coastal environment. The robust palette is limited to stained battened plywood and cedar, powdercoated aluminium, glass, hardwood and corrugated Colorsteel. • Exterior corrugated screens have been designed to slide over the lower level windows, wrapping the bach up when not in use.

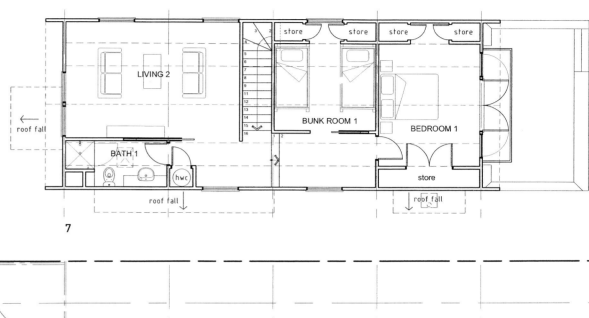

7

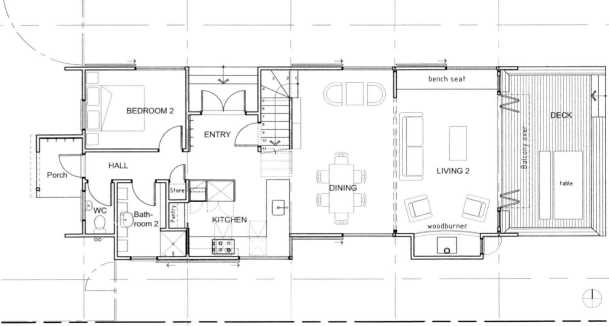

8

6

243

1

PUTNEY HOUSE

TONKIN ZULAIKHA GREER ARCHITECTS

This site is on the northern bank of the **Parramatta River**, which flows into **Sydney Harbour**. Set between large new houses of undistinguished design, its views are to the south. The plan takes the form of an enclosed and private north-facing courtyard with living rooms extending through the depth of the house. • The main living space is double-height. The expressive form of its folded plywood roof reaches through the wall to form a sunshade for its exposed glazing. On the upper floor, the main bedrooms and study are reached from a gallery bridge across the double-height space. • Externally the house has a dual character – to the north and the court, the forms are playful and expressive, while the southern riverfront elevation recalls a pure ideal of the classical villa, its three pavilions raised on a blank base. The external walls are grey-stained ply with aluminium tees between. Windows and solid shutters slide across the face of the walls, to leave the openings free of framing.

2

3

4

1   South façade looks out over the Parramatta River
2   External walls are grey-stained plywood with aluminium jointing strips
3   First floor plan
4   Ground floor plan

6

7

5 Folded ceiling of the living room extends though the glass as a sunshade
6 Living rooms open to the north court and to the river to the south
7 Gallery bridge crossing the living room with study beyond

Photography: Patrick Bingham-Hall

1

2

3

QUEENS PARK RESIDENCE

CULLEN FENG

This project involved a major alteration and addition to an existing semi-detached Federation-style cottage in **Sydney's Queens Park**. The original single-storey 'semi' had suffered various unsympathetic additions during the 1960s. • The front two rooms and the Alt Street façade of the house were salvaged, and the remainder demolished. The façade was stripped of its previous additions while the original timber detailing was reproduced and reinstated. • The front rooms were restored to their original design with detailed cornices, skirtings and mouldings. The original timber floorboards in these rooms were polished. A large room was added in the existing roof space with a new dormer window, giving the room a leafy outlook. • The rear of the house was rebuilt in contemporary style to accommodate kitchen/dining/living and a guest bathroom on the lower level. This opens up to a paved courtyard via large bifolding doors. On the upper level are two bedrooms, both with skylit ensuites and silver ash joinery. The rear bedroom has a semi-enclosed terrace that overlooks the courtyard. • A single-flight stair is concealed behind the kitchen joinery. It has a large translucent glazed wall to the north, which floods the upper levels with natural diffused light. The lower level of the new part of the house has high ceilings and a generous layout. • The kitchen has a long island bench of white reconstituted stone; the suspended rangehood in a custom enclosure is a dramatic form above. Limestone-toned large format tiles were used on the lower level, while a plush grey carpet was used on the upper level. The bathrooms feature silver ash joinery and rectangular white rectified wall tiles. • A double garage with a retreat space above is positioned at the rear of the site with access from the rear lane. The landscaping consists of concrete pavers, river pebbles and grassed areas. The garage wall facing the courtyard displays a stainless steel water feature.

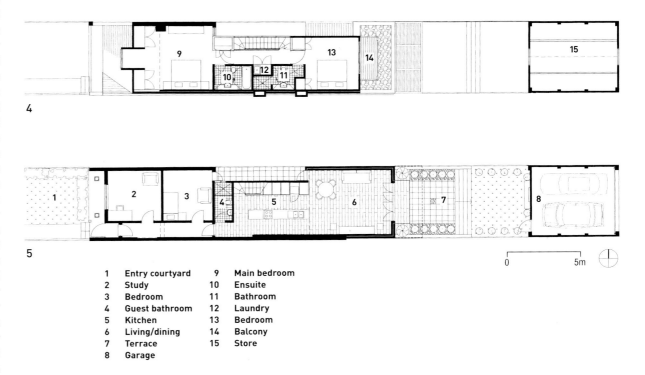

1	Entry courtyard	9	Main bedroom
2	Study	10	Ensuite
3	Bedroom	11	Bathroom
4	Guest bathroom	12	Laundry
5	Kitchen	13	Bedroom
6	Living/dining	14	Balcony
7	Terrace	15	Store
8	Garage		

1   Rear view of new two-storey addition
2   Bedroom with semi-enclosed balcony
3   View of kitchen with living area and courtyard beyond
4   First floor plan
5   Ground floor plan

6

7

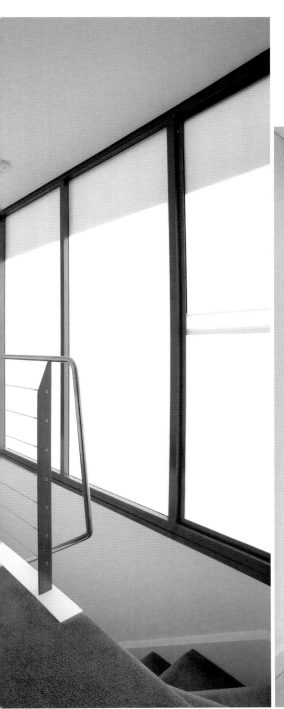

8

6   Bathroom
7   View of stair behind kitchen
8   View towards kitchen from dining/living area
    Photography: Murray Fredericks

1

RAGLAN STREET HOUSE

COY & YIONTIS ARCHITECTS

From the street, this 19th-century worker's cottage in an **inner Melbourne suburb** gives no hint of the strikingly contemporary residence behind its humble, heritage façade. The 244-square-metre building comprises three pavilions, separated by two external courtyards. • The façade and front two rooms of the original cottage have been retained and form a gatehouse to the new residence; the front rooms have been converted to a home office and a guest retreat and are isolated from the rest of the house by the first external courtyard. From there, a linear pond leads the eye into the main home. The water appears to pass under the living room floor and re-emerges in the second courtyard as a plunge pool, the line of the water offsetting the original central axis of the cottage. • An alternative approach to the traditional segregation of spaces has been explored with the internal and external volumes merging through the use of sliding glazed panels and a continuity of building materials. • Entering the main home via the second pavilion, the hardwood floor defining the entry and the kitchen gives way to travertine and a lower living and entertainment area. The third pavilion, the owners' private domain for living and sleeping, is the only multistorey section of the house and comprises a master bedroom, ensuite and walk-in robe upstairs and a laundry, garage and electronics workshop with a cellar below ground. • All significant internal living spaces have direct access to the outside, usually in the form of an entire wall pivoting or sliding away to link the two spaces and make them one. In the master ensuite, the entire ceiling is glazed to invite in the sky. In the study, the fully glazed southern aspect overlooks the pond and the courtyard. In each case, the sixth side of the cube defining the space has been consciously omitted to forge a link with the outside.

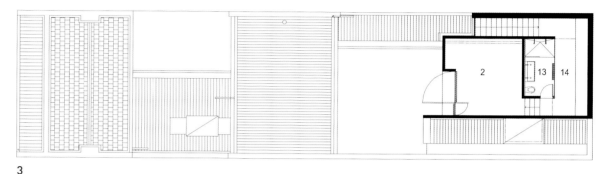

3

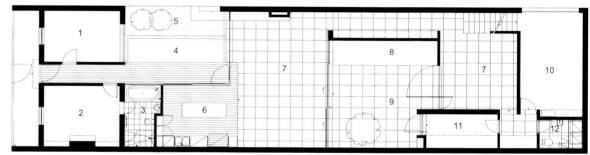

4

1	Study	9	Main courtyard
2	Bedroom	10	Garage
3	Bathroom	11	Workshop
4	Pond	12	Laundry
5	Entry courtyard	13	Ensuite
6	Kitchen	14	Walk-in robe
7	Living room	15	Cellar
8	Pool		

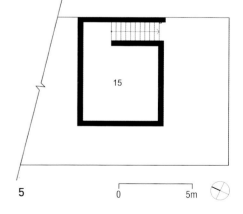

5

0   5m

2

1   View of main courtyard with open living spaces around
2   Kitchen and external entry passage, both on grey ironbark decking
3   First floor plan
4   Ground floor plan
5   Basement plan

6

7

8

9

Photography: Peter Clarke

10

RAMMED EARTH HOUSE

STEPHEN JOLSON ARCHITECT

This 465-square-metre, four-bedroom residence is located in **Flinders** on the **Mornington Peninsula**. With an integrated landscaped garden on a 40-hectare property, the project blurs the line between architecture, interior, landscape and furniture design. • Constructed predominantly in rammed earth, concrete and steel, the split-level house seemingly rises from the landscape and cranks to capture the sweeping rural and coastal panoramic views. The western elevation consists of solid rammed earth walls without penetrations, designed as thermal banks capturing the afternoon sun. The eastern elevation is glazed to siphon dominant views inside. • The large enclosed courtyard provides protection from gale-force winds, and allows northern sunlight to filter into the main living areas. Buffered from the main house by the courtyard is a self-contained sleeping and living zone, connected to the main house by a glazed link that can slide open to integrate the wet-edge pool and associated deck. • The hierarchy of the interior spaces is carefully articulated. Divided into two zones, main and guest, the house captures the dramatic coastal views and maximises solar amenity. A series of cranked and stepped modules follow the natural site contours and create a radial path that becomes the driveway and landscape gesture. Each module slices the view so that the landscape becomes a progression through the interior, in contrast to the 'wide-screen' panorama viewed upon arrival. The living spaces are open and informal to cater for a young growing family, and oriented to capture the morning and northern sunlight. • Each module in the main house is interconnected by the 'alley', a 25-metre corridor spine that binds the house together. By spacing the stepped transition between each module along the entirety of its length, the experience is reminiscent of a 'disappearing street'. A 'wedge' separates each module, and continues out into the landscape. Each wedge in the alley re-presents a slice of the view that is denied by the rammed earth walls. The effect is dramatic play of light and darkness that culminates in a framed view of the final glimpse of ocean on the site.

1	Entry
2	Courtyard
3	Glazed link
4	Lounge
5	Dining
6	Kitchen
7	Bedroom
8	Ensuite
9	Master bedroom
10	Study
11	Garage
12	Plant
13	Laundry
14	Powder room
15	Guest lounge
16	Pool
17	Driveway

1 Wet-edge pool
2 Floor plan
3 Arrival by car; view across ring-road and grass terraces to main residence

4

4   View of wet-edge pool from deck
5   Master bedroom with custom-designed bed from Australian hardwoods
6   View from lounge across pool
7   View back towards landscaped terraces
8   The 'alley' – feature corridor and spine through house

Photography: Scott Newett

5

6

7

8

1

2

3

RED ROCK LANE HOUSE

SHEPPARD & ROUT ARCHITECTS

This 329-square-metre home in **Redcliffs**, a suburb of **Christchurch**, was designed for a working couple and is located on a steep, north-facing sloping site in a sheltered valley with views out over the estuary to the ocean and city. • The entrance to the two-level house opens into a dramatic triple-height entry hall. This entry hall contains the stair linking the levels and on the outside, its white plastered vertical fin walls juxtapose and connect the black horizontal blocks. • These simple monopitched blocks are broken up with large windows and penetrations or projections in the walls. The upper floor is built into the hill while the lower floor decks float out over the land on steel frames. • The palette of colours and materials has been kept to a minimum with natural concrete blockwork, black stained weatherboards, black Colorsteel roof, green tinted glass windows and glass balustrades used on the exterior. The interior combines ground concrete, matai timber and wool carpet to the floors with white painted walls and glass ceramic or white tiles to the bathrooms. • The upper floor contains the master bedroom suite and an office for one of the occupants who works from home. The office provides views out to the north and is connected with the entry tower via a sliding shutter. The lower floor contains an open plan living/dining/kitchen space, projecting out over the land with internal laundry, back-up pantry and WC cut back into the hill. The guest facilities, comprising two bedrooms and a bathroom, are located off the open-plan space. • A narrow steel and glass balcony is suspended from the roof structure in front of the dining space. The glass doors on the western face of the living room open onto a terrace containing a built-in barbeque and spa pool. This area links to a cantilevered timber deck and swimming pool.

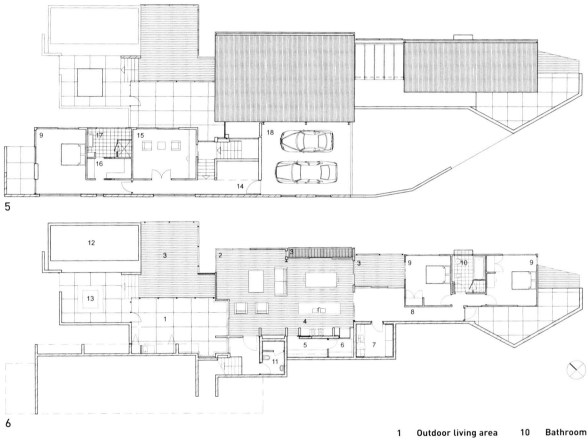

5

6

4

1	Outdoor living area	10	Bathroom
2	Living/dining	11	WC
3	Deck	12	Pool
4	Kitchen	13	Spa pool
5	Walk-in pantry	14	Entry
6	Wine cellar	15	Study
7	Laundry	16	Dressing
8	Hall	17	Ensuite
9	Bedroom	18	Garage

1 North view of house from road below

2 Outdoor eating area with study and master bedroom suite behind

3 Concrete terrace containing spa pool on west end of house steps down to wooden cantilevered deck and swimming pool

4 Terrazzo-topped kitchen bench and main dining/living space

5 Upper level floor plan

6 Lower level floor plan

7

7 Outdoor dining area contains built-in Teppanyaki barbeque, sink and refrigerator concealed behind bifold doors

8 Galvanised steel deck suspended from front of dining area on stainless steel rods

9 Double basin in master bedroom ensuite with full-height window and view to Pacific Ocean

10 Kitchen with island bench and walk-in pantry/preparation area and wine cellar accessed via sliding door

11 Stairwell in entry tower leading down to main living floor

Photography: Stephen Goodenough

8

9

10

11

1

2

3

REMUERA HOUSE

NOEL LANE ARCHITECTS

Located in **Remuera, Auckland**, at the head of a north-facing valley, this house site is overlooked by adjacent housing on the south and west, with native bush to the north and on the eastern slopes. The clients' three children occupy a three-unit development located alongside the northern boundary. • These very public citizens requested extreme privacy, while wishing to take maximum advantage of existing terraces and infrastructure, outlook and site aspect. • It initially seemed logical to renovate and extend the existing house, which had been owner-occupied for many years and previously altered and extended. In fact, it was rebuilt with only the existing swimming pool, tennis court, vehicle access ways and parking areas remaining intact. • This house is sculptured around function, using solids, voids and light to hold or release space, to invite or exclude. The spaces between solids form view and light shafts that pass through the living volume, connecting and separating them from each other, and in turn unifying the three-level structure into a single readable component for the occupier. Landscape elements are used similarly with exterior retaining walls and adjacent native bush areas, visually forming the house's exterior perimeter. • Art, sculpture, collectable furniture and sports memorabilia fill these volumes with many voices! This house is finely tuned to the specific needs of two very individual people.

1   North side of house: entrance
2   North side of house looking across swimming pool
3   East side of house looking across tennis court
4   Level three floor plan
5   Level two floor plan
6   Level one floor plan

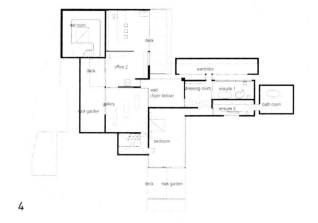

4

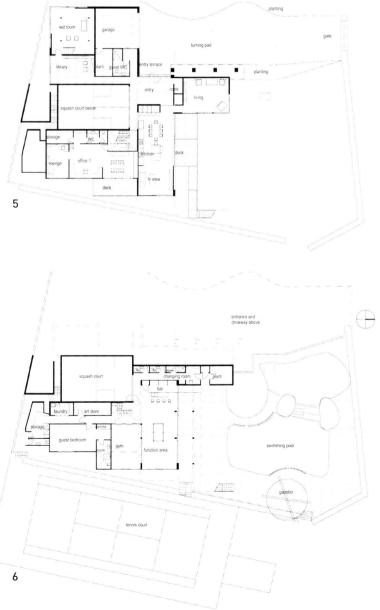

5

6

Photography: Simon Devitt

7

8

9

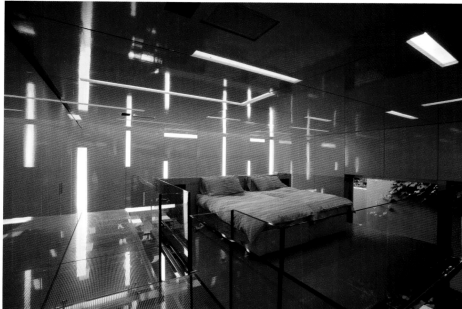

10

11

1

RETREAT HOUSE

BLACK KOSLOFF KNOTT ARCHITECTS

The site for this house on **Victoria's Mornington Peninsula** had been occupied for many years by a modest, fibro-cement shack that served as a summer holiday home. The original shelter embodied the spirit of beach weekends: simple, intimate spaces, organised around the living area. As the family grew, more space was required. • The clients sought a new home that would retain the best qualities of the original house and reflect a way of living quite different from their city life. This project explores ideas of temporary living and is a home designed around the routines of beach holidays and weekends. • The planning and siting of the residence was carefully considered. The L-shaped plan, with living and accommodation areas in separate wings, was oriented to screen views to neighbours on the south. This created a north-facing courtyard contained by the glazed living pavilion that maintains views along the length of the site to established stands of tea-tree and moonah. An internal timber deck corridor reinforces the axis, continuing outside to become a verandah to the accommodation wing. • Childhood memories of caravans and camping appealed: venturing outside to enter your bedroom or leaving the door open to the elements on a hot summer night. Consequently, living, kitchen and dining areas are grouped together as a communal 'mess hall' and bedrooms are clustered together in a linear, cabin-like plan. Bedrooms are nothing more than a place to sleep, with a simple rack to store clothes. The living space becomes the focus of the project, the social hub. • This project pays homage to the 1950's beach shacks that inhabit the area. Retreat House is a simple and efficient structure that celebrates the routines and rituals of the beach holiday.

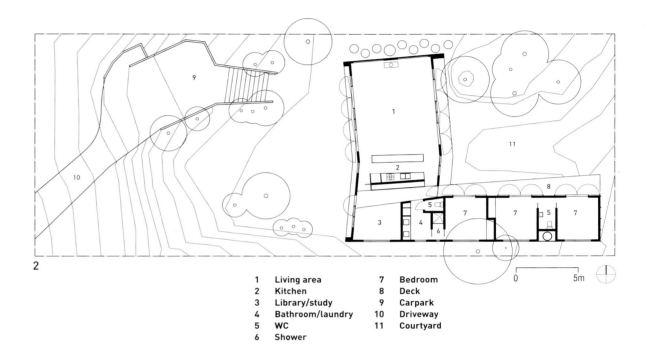

1	Living area	7	Bedroom
2	Kitchen	8	Deck
3	Library/study	9	Carpark
4	Bathroom/laundry	10	Driveway
5	WC	11	Courtyard
6	Shower		

1   Oblique view of cranked façade
2   Site and floor plan
3   Night view to main living space

4   Accommodation wing from internal courtyard
5   West façade and front lawn
6   View to courtyard from main living space
Photography: Shannon McGrath

4

5

6

1

RICHMOND HOUSE

WOLVERIDGE ARCHITECTS

Located at the eastern end of a newly developed tract of land overlooking **Richmond's Burnley Park**, this house is constructed over three levels for a family of five on a 160-square-metre site. • The logical sequence of accommodation was to provide two bedrooms for the sons with their own private space to hang out in at the ground level. The living areas span the first floor and are built around a private north-facing deck. The emphasis of the floor plan is around this outdoor space, which is a hideaway and provides natural light into the building. The parents' and daughter's bedrooms are located on the top floor and turn their back on the street as do the lower floors. • All living areas share views of the park. These spaces are flooded with morning sun. A kitchen window over Albert Place allows the residents to see who's coming down the street and provides cross-ventilation to the building. • A rendered form at the middle level dominates the structure. It hangs over the entry and is immediately visible upon entering Albert Place. This form hovers over a pedestrian track and continues to the east elevation where it becomes a freestanding element in reducing visual bulk. • Areas that require privacy, such as the master ensuite, are clad in a fixed aluminium louvre screen. At ground level, the same material provides the initial point of security. In warm weather, the front door can remain open, creating a breezeway into the house. • The shiplap form of the western red cedar cladding continues to the roof, encompasses the structure and returns to the private outdoor space, providing a natural element at the human scale.

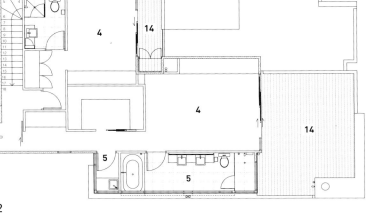

2

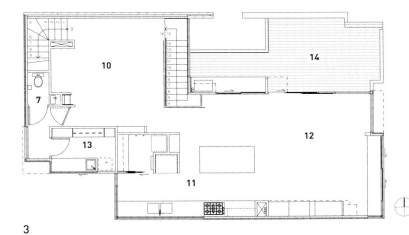

3

1	Entry
2	Bike store
3	Chill out
4	Bedroom
5	Bathroom
6	Court
7	WC
8	Garage
9	Store
10	Dining
11	Kitchen
12	Living
13	Laundry
14	Deck

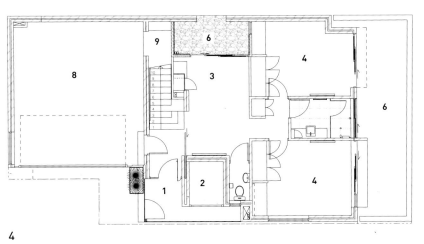

4

1   Southeast view from park
2   Second floor plan
3   First floor plan
4   Ground floor plan

5

6

5   First-floor north deck
6   Kitchen from living area
7   Stairwell at entry
8   View into north deck from living area
Photography: Shannon McGrath

RIVERVIEW RESIDENCE

MELOCCO & MOORE ARCHITECTS

The site is on the edge of a valley that feeds into **Tambourine Bay**, on the north side of Sydney Harbour. The central idea of the project was to create an environment that would house a series of dynamic internal spaces, providing display opportunities for the client's extensive art collection and offering a continual journey of discovery for the occupant. This was combined with the client's wish to engage with the magnificent trees on and surrounding the site. • The building steps down the site in response to the slope and existing vegetation. From the street the building creates a backdrop to the enormous split trunk of an angophora gum tree, with simple openings to either side. The upper portion of the dwelling provides differing pedestrian and vehicular entry sequences that allow the visitor to appreciate the magnificent spread of the gums. The changing volumes along the entry sequence hint at the variety of spaces in the project, revealed only as the occupant passes through the residence. The building reveals itself slowly along the central spine, opening up into living areas to the north and closing down to private areas to the south. • The design solution enhances views of the trees without compromising privacy and western solar issues. Two pavilions, with living areas to the north and more private spaces to the south, flank the central entry. This program is maintained over each of the three levels and staggered ceiling and floor planes provide opportunities to articulate the space. A series of brick blade walls run down the hill, bisecting the site and separating bedroom and living spaces. Springing from these walls, separate skillion roofs provide passive solar access to all sections of the building. External decks and courtyards create varied internal–external connections.

1   Rear view
2   Roof plan
3   Ground floor plan
4   Lower ground floor plan

1   Entrance area
2   Kitchen
3   Dining
4   Living
5   Bedroom
6   Bathroom
7   Study
8   Cellar
9   Carport
10 Laundry

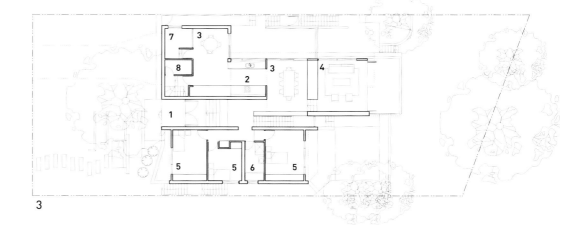

2

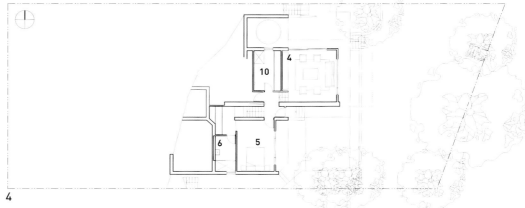

3

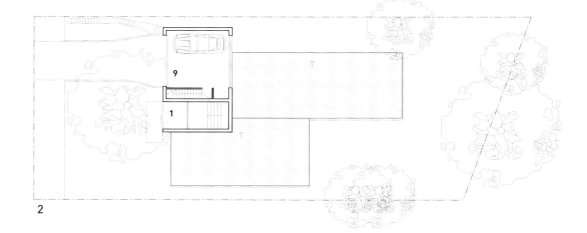

4

5

6

7

8

9

10

5   Deck off the kitchen, one of many deck areas
6   Bathroom adjacent to the main bedroom
7   View from street
8   Living room
9   Entrance vestibule with the front garden in the distance
10   Kitchen and dining area

Photography: Paul Gosney

1

2

3

1 Sculptural stair hovers in shimmering reflectivity
2 Landscaped internal courtyard provides an urban oasis
3 Light filled, open-plan living articulated by texture, colour and form
4 Urban renewal: a derelict warehouse transformed
5 Translucent glass adds mystery and light to the floating bathroom
6 First floor plan
7 Ground floor plan

Photography: Pru Taylor (1–3); Judith North/
Neville Cowland (4,5)

ROSE SPRING APARTMENTS

COWLAND NORTH PTY LTD

Built before 1920, the existing building was a textile manufacturing plant until its functional shift began in 1999. • The redevelopment is a skilful, sensitive integration of the old warehouse shell with a more contemporary interpretation of industry. Key to this purpose was to create apartments that were energy efficient and used low embodied energy materials. • While the evidence of the new life of the building does not readily reveal itself to the outside viewer, it is on the inside – where the remnants of the building's past reflect upon the new spaces within – that a rich and unique sense of place and time is created. • The newly formed airy apartments are centred around a bright white courtyard. The light and gregarious space was created by the removal of a section of the existing roof, providing the residents with an internal/external oasis. • Limestone party walls frame each apartment, providing a sophisticated, low-maintenance backdrop to the spaces. The emphasis is upon large, well-defined, functional spaces punctuated by existing structural elements and floors that 'float' into the volume, forming heights from a cosy 2.1 metres to a soaring 6 metres – a vitality of scale and space at every turn. Stairs hover as functional sculpture – glass balustrades offer function and visual dynamism, counterpointed by the recycled Australian blue gum treads. Translucent glass walls and black steel offer fineness and strength to define the upper bedrooms and bathrooms from the living spaces below while allowing light to shimmer throughout.

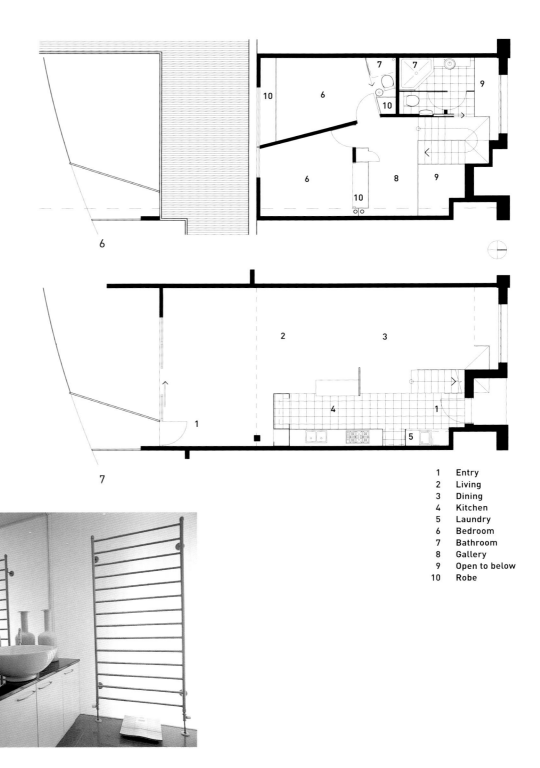

1	Entry
2	Living
3	Dining
4	Kitchen
5	Laundry
6	Bedroom
7	Bathroom
8	Gallery
9	Open to below
10	Robe

4

5

1

2

3

4

5

ROSENEATH HOUSE

NOVAK & MIDDLETON ARCHITECTS

Located on a spectacular site overlooking **Oriental Bay** and beyond to **Wellington** and the harbour, this house sits in harmony and in contrast with its dramatic location. • The owners' brief requested a contemporary New Zealand home that responded to the dramatic and variable environment, providing a sense of shelter yet a connection to the landscape. Quality of space and light were essential concerns, as were privacy and security. The house was designed in close collaboration with the clients, whose backgrounds in architecture and the arts were instrumental in developing and refining the project to the highest level. • The house was required to maximise the view, provide a high degree of privacy, and to showcase the clients' collection of contemporary art. A large painting by artist Stephen Bambury was commissioned. The requirement that it be displayed in a prominent position away from direct sunlight influenced the design of the three-storey central stairway atrium. • The palette of materials is restrained: zinc, aluminium, bluestone, concrete, plaster and timber comprise the materials throughout the house. The house is modern and minimalist, designed to provide a comfortable and functional environment for family living.

7

6

1   Outdoor terrace with concrete table overlooking Wellington Harbour
2   Spectacular hilltop location
3   Wine cellar
4   Front entry and stairwell with living area beyond
5   Raised kitchen with polished concrete blocks
6   The house presents its private side to the street
7   Exterior materials of zinc, concrete and plaster continue into the interior

Photography: Todd Crawford Photography (1–5); Simon Novak (6,7)

1

2

3

4

SAID HOUSE

DESIGN KING COMPANY

The 450-square-metre Said House is located on a prominent and restricted corner block in the harbourside suburb of **Vaucluse** in **Sydney's eastern suburbs**. It was designed for a family of five with a large extended family. The brief included four bedrooms and study, large and interconnected living spaces, pool, spa and extended covered terraces. • Through the use of layering stone-clad walls, columns and openings, the architect has sought to achieve a sense of privacy and seclusion. While achieving a real sense of enclosure, the layering of the design also allows the home to capture light and views from the nearby harbour. • Subtle offsets in the plan and changes in level give a sense of individuality to each space while maintaining an essentially open plan. The stairs leading to the upper level are backed by a bank of stone basalt. Light from the glazing above washes down into the stairwell. • The sculptural use of stone and concrete dominates the building while the careful use of recycled timbers and metal detailing counterpoints the mass, which in turn creates a sense of timelessness and modernity. • The lighting, furnishing, finishes and services were all carefully designed and chosen to reinforce and complement this raw and direct aesthetic. The building has a wonderful sense of scale, light and acoustic quality that creates a unique atmosphere. • Jon King has produced a highly crafted building that deftly combines a strong sense of raw muscularity with a highly tuned sense of materials, creating an environment that is reassuring, tranquil and visually stimulating.

5

6

1   The light-filled dining room and its luxurious 16-seat dining table
2   The masonry boundary wall and associated planting create a haven from the street
3   Feature window linking garden to lounge room
4   Polished concrete stairs lead past the stone basalt to entry door
5   An indoor–outdoor terrace which can be opened to, or protected from, the elements
6   The indoor terrace with open fireplace and heated bluestone paving

Photography: Brett Boardman

1

2

3

4

SEATOUN HOUSE

HERRIOT + MELHUISH ARCHITECTURE

On a reasonably exposed corner site, within walking distance to the beach in **Seatoun, Wellington**, a house was required to replace a villa that was destroyed by fire. • Differing materials were used to define the various programmatic elements of the house. Kitchen, dining, living and bedrooms were contained in the dominant building form, a dark-stained, timber-clad element open to the north. Meanwhile, to the south, services, garage and den were housed in a closed concrete mass, dug into the ground to form an adjacent courtyard. Finally, a double-height glazed metal box links and interconnects these two elements, the transparency signalling entry and drawing natural light into the house. • To maximise outdoor living, the timber box was pulled back from the north and east boundaries, and the concrete box drawn away from the west. This created a series of distinct outdoor spaces arrayed about the house. • To the north, a 'soft' grassed area was opened towards the sun, while remaining protected from the southerly winds. A series of sliding doors open up the north face of the house, creating a continuity between indoor and outdoor living. • East of the timber box, a harder paved area was constructed for morning use. Again, the house was opened up to the outside, this time via cantilevered bifolding windows that concertina away the entire corner. Finally, a sunken paved courtyard connects to the den through glazed sliding doors. This courtyard remains protected from northwest winds while enjoying maximum exposure to the afternoon sun.

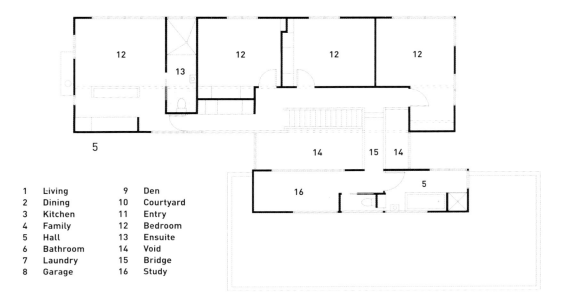

1	Living	9	Den
2	Dining	10	Courtyard
3	Kitchen	11	Entry
4	Family	12	Bedroom
5	Hall	13	Ensuite
6	Bathroom	14	Void
7	Laundry	15	Bridge
8	Garage	16	Study

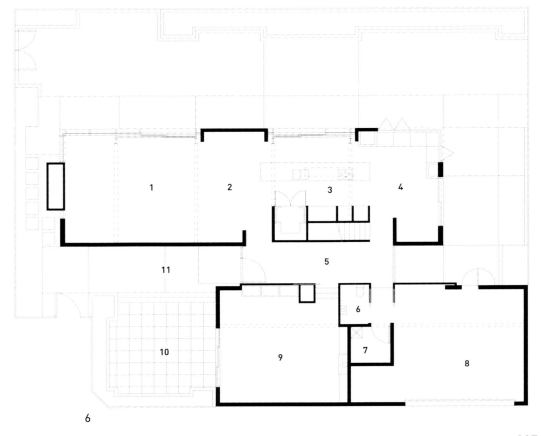

1   Double-height, glazed entry interconnects main living spaces housed in timber box with the more solid concrete mass containing the service functions
2   View of west elevation from street
3   View from kitchen to living room
4   Main living area
5   First floor plan
6   Ground floor plan

Photography: Tim Lovell

1

2

SENTINEL

GILES TRIBE ARCHITECTS

Sentinel is a 300-square-metre family home located on **Sugarloaf Bay** in **Castlecrag, Sydney**. The design merges city living and a magnificent waterfront bushland setting with architecture that celebrates the site's uniqueness. • The brief was for a substantial family home that included open-plan living areas, parents' retreat, children's bedrooms, home office or guest accommodation and entertaining areas. The objective was to create a unique home that maximises the opportunity afforded by the water and bush views. • Two buildings are linked by a glazed lobby: one addresses the street and accommodates the garage and studio; the other addresses the water and includes separate zones for parents, living, sleeping and casual entertaining. The main façade of the house creates a wall, which conceals the view and setting that lie beyond. Circulation through the house is a journey of varied spatial experiences, intimate and expansive vistas and connections to water. The theme of water is developed through the outdoor spaces and landscaping and through the seamless connection from the indoors to the harbour beyond. • The principal living level is at the heart of the house, with the bedroom levels and connections to ground separated by only one level. Extensive terraces with frameless glass balustrades and expansive openings further integrate indoor and outdoor living. • The contemporary aesthetic was developed from the expression of horizontal and vertical planes and screens. Large-scale masonry walls protect from the elements while low pitched roofs with broad overhangs, deep reveals, automated louvred pergolas and vertical screens modulate the sun, frame views and control privacy. • The calm, minimal interior is created by a limited palette of materials in contrast to the ruggedness of the natural landscape. The architecture and interior design are integrated, each reinforcing the intention to create a house that is both visually beautiful and wonderful to inhabit.

4

3

5

1   The juxtaposition of horizontal and vertical elements is evident in the street façade
2   A glazed entry lobby traverses the rock outcrop and provides separation between the main house and the home office/studio
3   Walls to the terraces can be fully opened to create a seamless flow between inside and outside
4   The living areas blur the distinction between indoors and out, with the pool merging with the bushland and harbour beyond
5   The house was designed as a series of terraces, which respond to the steeply sloping site

Photography: Brett Boardman

SERESIN HOUSE

PETE BOSSLEY ARCHITECTS

This project, encompassing a house, guest house, shed and boatshed is in **Waterfall Bay**. This intimate tidal bay is part of the Marlborough Sounds, at the northern end of the South Island of New Zealand. • The site for the new house is adjacent to the jetty, tucked onto a narrow sliver of land between the sea and the rising hills behind. It was important that existing trees be maintained, which meant that that lower levels had to be cut into the bank to reduce the impact of the overall form. Arrival to the site is normally by sea to the jetty, so the double-height glazed stair space reflects the axis of the arrival sequence, while the entry path zigzags off the axis and then returns. • The house has two elements: the two-storey main wing with guest bedrooms below and living rooms above, and an upper-level main bedroom which is linked by a cranked and rising glazed bridge, under which the landscape falls towards the sea. This bedroom reaches out over the bank into the tall beech trees, supported by a collection of leaning posts suggesting an instability and sense of movement appropriate to the owner's lifestyle. A concrete fireplace is expressed on the outside of the otherwise timber box, to further suggest the sense of imbalance. • In order to create a sense of comfort and avoid a brittle 'newness', wide floorboards, which will quickly age, were combined with a variety of plywood linings, demolition hardwood beams and columns, and timber joinery. The house is beautifully 'inhabited' by a collection of fine, well-worn, mainly mid 20th-century furniture and light fittings. A variety of window proportions and positions ensures an interesting range of connections to the sea immediately below, and to the mid-distance views across the bay.

3

2

Opposite:
The beautiful stair floats in an atrium of recycled bridge timbers
2   Main bedroom projects into the existing trees
3   Upper level floor plan

4   Main bedroom on 'walking posts' is linked to the house by the glazed bridge
5   A variety of heights and volumes articulates the different interior spaces
6   The eclectic collection of fine furniture complements the relaxed nature of the house
7   Main ensuite offers superb views of the bay
8   Main bedroom with fireplace and bay beyond

Photography: Paul McCredie

4

5

6

7

8

1

2

3

4

SHENTON PARK RESIDENCE

CRAIG STEERE ARCHITECTS

Overlooking the serene **Shenton Park Lake** near **Perth**, this contemporary two-storey, 422-square-metre residence has been designed to maximise its outlook and feeling of space, while maintaining individual privacy. • The front courtyards and ground floor level have been raised above footpath level to provide a natural height barrier and buffer for visual privacy from the street. The open plan layout of the downstairs living spaces helps achieve maximum exposure to the lake from all parts of the ground floor. Blade wing walls provide privacy and isolation from the adjoining properties, framing cinematographic views of the lake and capturing the warm northern sun in winter. • Greenery and water features complement the natural connection with the lake. Upstairs, the bedrooms appear to float within the tree canopies, with fully glazed bi-folding walls opening to the park via cantilevering 'green' balconies over its setting. • At the front of the upper floor sit the main suite and support rooms, providing the intimacy of a hotel suite for the owner. The bedroom opens onto the park via full-height bi-folding glass doors that extend across the full length of the balcony. The soaring balcony disguises the street below, complemented by the solid planter bringing the greenery into the bedroom. • With the orientation of the street boundary to the north and front of the park, the opportunity existed to exploit the northern façade to access the warm northern winter sun. This northern exploitation was further demonstrated by designing a central outdoor living facility at the front of the property, which presents full visual access to the park and ease of flow to and from the ground-floor living spaces. An electronically operable fabric roof provides adjustable solar control. • A large cantilevered roof overhangs the northern façade, which not only regulates the summer and winter sun but also complements the blade walls to frame the view of the park.

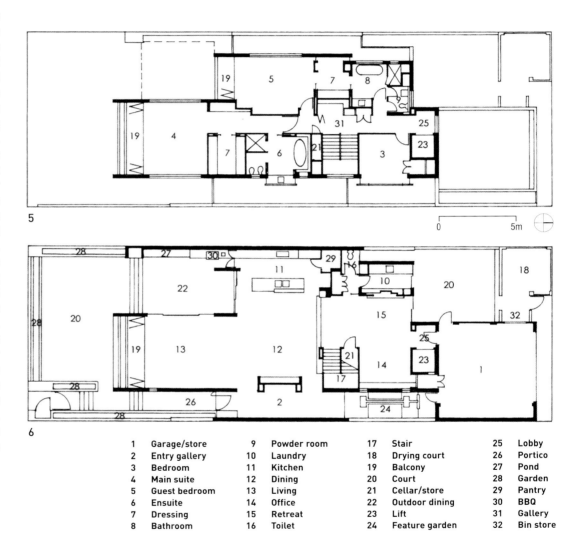

1	Garage/store	9	Powder room	17	Stair	25	Lobby
2	Entry gallery	10	Laundry	18	Drying court	26	Portico
3	Bedroom	11	Kitchen	19	Balcony	27	Pond
4	Main suite	12	Dining	20	Court	28	Garden
5	Guest bedroom	13	Living	21	Cellar/store	29	Pantry
6	Ensuite	14	Office	22	Outdoor dining	30	BBQ
7	Dressing	15	Retreat	23	Lift	31	Gallery
8	Bathroom	16	Toilet	24	Feature garden	32	Bin store

1 View from entry gallery to portico and living room
2 Northeast view
3 Views from outside through living room to dining area and retreat beyond
4 View from living and dining through to kitchen
5 Upper floor plan
6 Ground floor plan

Photography: Robert Frith, Acorn Photo Agency

1

2

3

4

5

SMALL STREET RESIDENCE

KEVIN HAYES ARCHITECTS PTY LTD

The Small Street Residence is located on a narrow lane in the **Brisbane suburb of New Farm**. Traditionally, these lanes were used for servicing the rear of the houses; more recently, with the increase in urban density in the inner city of Brisbane, they are coming to life with a series of new house forms. • The major design principle for this 190-square-metre house was a play between the inside and outside. Voids are used throughout to create a sense of drama, light and connection from higher levels to lower levels, inside to outside and through the living spaces. Large openings and oversized louvres are used to give a sense of permeability and to provide a strong relationship with the outdoor spaces. Built-in furniture, 'external' materials, such as stone and timber battening, and water features are used internally to evoke a sense of outdoors in the living areas. • Materials were selected to be stimulating and evocative. A deliberate play between more traditional elements, such as the Queensland 'timber and tin', and later post-war development, such as the use of masonry, were used in conjunction with more modern elements to create an interface of old and new. • Sustainability was an important consideration in the design of the house. The 'snorkel' sculptural element draws light and air into the interior. Large scale, high-level windows provide passive ventilation and timber batten screens filter natural light down to the lower levels, creating a play of shadow and light inside the house. Passive cooling is provided in the form of large overhangs and the retention of a significant tree to shade the house. • The experience of entry and the play of journey were crafted through a large, highly defined and private entry to the cool sanctity of the dwelling. This quiet privacy is in practical contrast to the transparent staircase, which presents vignettes of circulation and journey to the streetscape, while maintaining the privacy of the destination spaces.

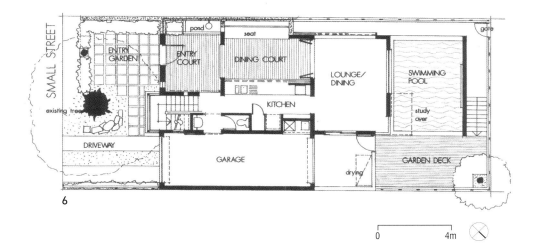

6

1　Mango tree leading to entry gate in stone wall
2　Rear of house showing the 'snorkel' and the relationship between house and pool
3　Dining area with built-in seat/screen; kitchen to right
4　Study cantilevering over pool with floor window looking down on water
5　Entry area with internal water feature
6　Ground floor plan
7　Kitchen opens out to entry court and double-height dining area

Photography: Exposure Photographers Pty Ltd (1,3,5,7); Gerard Lynch (2,4)

7

SOUTH PADDINGTON RESIDENCE

CULLEN FENG

This project involved a major alteration and addition to an existing terrace house in **Paddington**, in **inner-city Sydney**. • Being in a heritage-listed area, it was important for the streetscape that the original façade was restored to its former glory. Thus the various unsympathetic additions such as the enclosed balcony, the masonry fence and mosaic entry tiles were removed. The balcony and front fence were reinstated in reproduction iron lace, timber shutters were added to the windows and sandstone pavers were used for the entry porch. • The site is long and narrow, and also has a slope from the front to the rear lane of more than 3 metres. The rear of the house was demolished, and rebuilt in a contemporary style over two levels. The volume made available by the slope to the rear was used for a double garage, the roof of which forms an elevated deck. This forms the main outdoor living space which has more privacy and outlook at this level. • The living/dining space has high ceilings and an open kitchen. The kitchen has stainless steel benches, polyurethane cupboards and a glass splashback. Karri timber floorboards were used downstairs, while chocolate brown carpet was used on the upper level. • The Victorian front rooms on the lower level were converted into a media room and bathroom respectively. The upper-level bedrooms feature custom polyurethane joinery. The main bedroom balcony has a perforated steel panel balustrade, a material typically used for industrial platform flooring. The balcony also has an external blind; a folding arm awning is used to shade the living room glazing below. • The landscaping consists of weathered timber decking and concrete pavers, with ziggurat-style hardwood planters. At the end of the deck is a mirror stainless water wall.

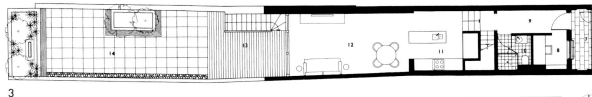

1	Balcony	9	Hallway
2	Main bedroom	10	Guest bath
3	Robe	11	Kitchen
4	Bathroom	12	Living/dining
5	Bedroom	13	Terrace
6	Balcony	14	Terrace
7	Entry porch	15	Garage
8	Study	16	Store

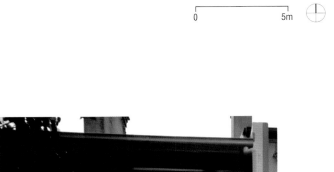

2

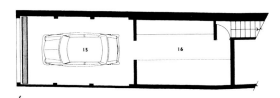

3

4

0   5m

1   Courtyard with custom planters and mirror stainless water feature
2   First floor plan
3   Ground floor plan
4   Basement floor plan
5   Restored Victorian façade

5

6   Kitchen with stainless steel island bench
7   Bathroom
8   Living area with courtyard beyond
9   Rear view of new two-storey addition

Photography: Murray Fredericks

7

8

9

1

SPRING STREET APARTMENT

FORM ARCHITECTURE FURNITURE

The brief was the refurbishment of an early 1970's apartment on the seventh floor of a building that was one of the first apartment blocks built in **Melbourne**. The building has a prime position, next to the Windsor Hotel and diagonally opposite Parliament House and the Treasury building, but the apartment itself was in poor condition. The existing slab of the 174-square-metre apartment had sagged in the middle over its 30 years, and the existing bathroom and ensuite layouts required substantial alteration to improve their efficiency. • The challenge was to enhance the views to Melbourne's east and to open up and refit the interior, as well as providing an additional optional bedroom and study area. • The key design idea was to define spaces for use without closing them off from the view or the rest of the apartment. This was achieved by the use of two timber-slatted screens. A third articulated fan screen is finished in rock maple veneer. This trackless screen slides on a radial trajectory to enclose the study area and screen it from the living area. • A curved bulkhead further defines the dining area, and allows the use of more expressive lighting. A bar with pendant lights was incorporated into the kitchen and a venting rangehood was installed to accommodate the client's request for an indoor barbeque. The parquetry floor reinforces and minimises the entry and traffic areas and enhances the curves of the fixed screen.

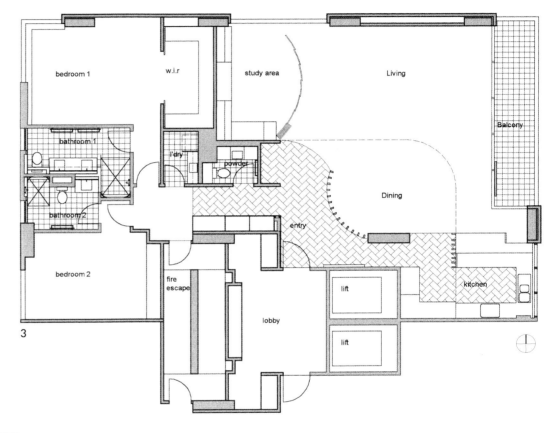

3

2

1 View to kitchen from living area with Melbourne's Treasury building beyond
2 View across dining to living room and balcony. Entertainment unit designed by Tony Stuart.
3 Floor plan

4

5

6

7

8

9

10

Photography: Dan Magree, The Bakehouse Studio

1   Curved façade
2   Shadow lines emphasise the tilting panels of the back elevation
3   Skylight void above living room ceiling
4   First floor plan
5   Ground floor plan
6   Lower ground floor plan

1

2

SPRY HOUSE

DURBACH BLOCK ARCHITECTS

The brief for Spry House was big for its site, resembling in a way a public rather than private commission. The site had an overwhelming view of **Sydney Harbour** that influenced every architectural move. So a primary question became: should the house be parallel or perpendicular to that view? The architects' preference was for the latter, with its more ambivalent relationship to the harbour; this scheme with three fluid and interweaved bands short-ending the view was the result. • It was decided to locate a large part of the brief (extra bedrooms and bathrooms, storage) within a base, on which the rest of the reduced mass of the house could be built. In this way a large clear platform, flush with the street on one side and raised on the other side, was constructed to take advantage of the views. • The intention was to make the building cloud-like, shading the living podium. Not a modernist box that hovers despite the obvious weight, but a floating mass that actually looks light enough to be there. Not at all improbable. • As the clients' accommodation requirements increased, the roof became thicker and thicker as it became more habitable. Fissures and courts were cut through the roof not only to reveal its depth, but also to receive more light, cross views and air into the living podium. The timber and glass façade here makes the wall appear impossibly delicate and ephemeral. The thinnest windows imaginable emit fleeting flickering pure green light blades throughout the space.

1	Lower entry
2	Bedroom 3
3	Laundry
4	Study
5	Store
6	Sauna
7	Bathroom
8	Bedroom 4
9	Living
10	Dining
11	Courtyard
12	Guest WC
13	Kitchen
14	Garage
15	Master bedroom balcony
16	Master bedroom
17	Dressing room
18	Bathroom
19	Guest bedroom
20	Guest bathroom
21	Herb garden

7

8

9

10

7   View of the harbour from pool
8   Connection of internal living spaces
9   Top of skylight
10   View of living spaces from entry stair
11   View of courtyard from underneath

Photography: Anthony Browell (1–3,9–11); Brett Boardman (7,8)

11

1   Rear showing landscaping around the pool
2   Corner window looking into living area
3   Front elevation
4   Front of house with double garage
5   First floor plan
6   Ground floor plan

STRATHMORE HOUSE

BBP ARCHITECTS

The brief for this project in suburban **Melbourne** was the refurbishment of an existing brick residence, including the addition of a new first-floor bedroom wing and family bathroom. The intent of the new design was to create spatial interest through the subtle manipulation of the cube in plan and section, thus redefining the original order of the home. The principal aims were to create as much living space as practically possible and to maximise natural light throughout the residence. Solar orientation and the ability of the building to naturally ventilate were other important factors in the planning of the building. • The existing ground floor was refurbished to incorporate a contemporary open plan family/kitchen dining area, a study, a master bedroom wing and all associated amenities. While the existing infrastructure of the original building was suitable for reuse, the intent was to 'wrap' and redefine the existing building both in plan, section and built form to create a new contemporary language to the building. • Internal spaces and finishes were kept simple, to heighten the experience of the house and its relationship to the environment and setting. The use of minimal materials such as glass, steel and metal cladding results in a building which is primarily made up of a series of basic square boxes, partially supported on a light structure and partially engaging with the site. • The building delicately terraces up the sloping site with the ground level horizontally framing views to the gardens. While maintaining ordered forms, the building has a transparency through the contrasts of solids, voids and openings. The building represents a lightness through the intentional expression of structure and acknowledges the theory of 'less is more'. It is a bold response to the site and the views through the house clearly reinforce the importance of the relationships between internal and external space.

1   Bedroom 3
2   Bathroom
3   Bedroom 2
4   Void
5   Lounge
6   Dining
7   Kitchen
8   Entry
9   Laundry
10 Store
11 Study
12 Powder room
13 Ensuite
14 Bedroom 1
15 Robe
16 Carport

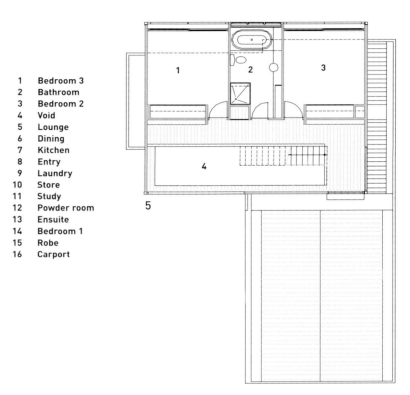

5

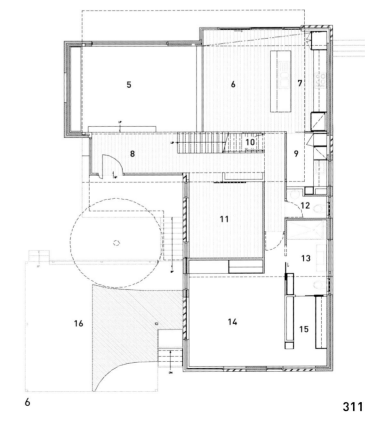

6

4

7

9

8

7   Rear of house and swimming pool
8   Living area looking into dining space
9   Blackbutt timber flooring to staircase with frameless balustrade
10 Living area with fireplace
11 Bedroom with bookcase
Photography: Chris Ott

10

11

1

TAMARAMA HOUSE

MORGAN DICKSON ARCHITECTURE (ARCHITECT);
ARCHITECT PRINEAS (INTERIORS)

Perched in the dress circle of **Sydney's Tamarama**, this home creates a contemporary environment in which to enjoy the beach. Working within an approved building envelope, the design intention was to control the mass of the building. This has been achieved through the fragmentation of discrete building elements. The sandstone plinth housing the garage and internal access to the house creates a large terrace fronting onto the park with beach views beyond. • Two masonry boxes express their functions from the outside. A solid service core including the kitchen, laundry and bathrooms runs along the east side of the building. The living spaces have a direct connection to the front terrace and the rear north-facing courtyard. Bi-fold doors blur the line between inside and out and expose the home to sunlight and natural ventilation. • The bathrooms have been designed simply, so that fixtures hang from the walls, allowing a large bathroom space. Storage is built in as cabinets on the walls which sit between the long slot windows above and below. At night, joinery up- and down-lights create a similar lighting effect – the cabinetry appears to float on the wall. • The kitchen configures as a white joinery unit with subtle variation in materials and textures. The large stone island bench has been designed to double as an informal dining area. Opening out onto a sunny rear courtyard, there is direct access to the barbeque area and outdoor dining. • Upstairs, a custom-designed bed sits in the main bedroom facing the view. Side tables are integrated in the design. A long pendant floats over the centre of each of the side tables, completing the composition of the tall bed head. • The artificial lighting strategy throughout the house has been designed to complement the solar design of the architecture. Recessed up-lights throw light onto the ceiling at night creating an ambient glow, while strategically placed spotlights attract attention to feature artworks and sculptures throughout the house.

1	Garage
2	Subfloor storage
3	Cellar
4	Subfloor
5	Plant room
6	Entry
7	Dining
8	Side passage
9	Laundry/WC
10	Bath
11	Kitchen
12	Courtyard
13	Family
14	Bedroom 2
15	Bedroom 3
16	Lounge
17	Lower terrace
18	Path
19	Void
20	Ensuite
21	Walk-in robe
22	Balcony
23	Bedroom 1
24	Sunroom
25	Terrace
26	Roof garden

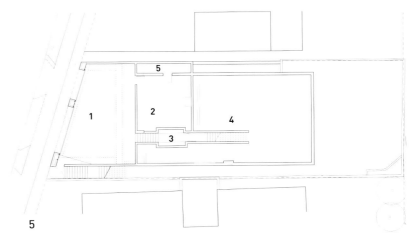

1 A solid sandstone plinth anchors the house to the ground, creating a terrace that overlooks the beach
2 View from the sunny, north-facing rear courtyard
3 Level three floor plan
4 Level two floor plan
5 Level one floor plan

6   Bi-fold doors slide away, creating a seamless transition from the family area and kitchen to the rear courtyard
7   A custom-designed bed and sideboard furnish the main bedroom
8   The kitchen island bench doubles as an informal eating area
9   A generous ensuite connects to the main bedroom
10 The lounge area of the front terrace has an eclectic mix of furniture including French antiques and 20th-century classics

Photography: Brett Boardman

6

9

10

8

1

2

3

TEA-TREE HOUSE

MADDISON ARCHITECTS

This house, in **Flinders** on the **Mornington Peninsula**, was designed as a holiday house for an extended family to occupy over short periods of time. Due to a tight budget, its size was contained to a modest 228 square metres on a site of 2000 square metres. It was rationalised that the house could be separated into two separate volumes; a two-storey square box dedicated to sleeping, and a single-storey rectangular box for 'living'. The two boxes are connected by a slender link. • The activities zones are separated into two volumes, acting as acoustic isolators. The children are accommodated in the bunkroom with their own entertainment facilities, and the living area is used as a space for the adults. Sisal has been applied on the ceiling, contributing to the containment of noise throughout. • A predominantly lightweight timber-constructed house was considered to be the most achievable for minimising the cost and speed of construction. This lightweight construction and contained footprint recalls the 1960's fibro holiday shack. • The use of tea-tree battens formed the basis of the initial design. A locally sourced material, often used as fencing for coastal properties, it has been applied here in a random manner to the top and sides of the decks, acting as a privacy screen in which the dappled light evokes the notion of a relaxed seaside setting complete with barbeque. The non-linear nature of the tea-tree battens breaks down the clean lines of the refined linear boxes, while the decks extend the perceived size of the internal living spaces. • The house celebrates the modesty of a beach shack with its use of materials and the contained footprint, celebrating the ideals of a relaxed weekend residence.

1 Deck
2 Living
3 Dining
4 Kitchen
5 Bathroom
6 Bedroom
7 Bunkroom
8 Void

0   5m

1   Double-storey sleeping module and single-storey living module
2   Stair in link
3   Living and dining interior
4   First floor plan
5   Ground floor plan
6   Night on northern deck

Photography: Rhiannon Slatter

1

1   Glamorous resort-style swimming pool and entertaining area
2   Dining area with custom-designed 3-metre-long Macassar ebony timber table
3   Floor plan
4   Glossy white kitchen with concealed appliances

2

TOORAK RESIDENCE

DAVID HICKS PTY LTD

In this refurbishment of a two-storey home in the **Melbourne suburb of Toorak**, an orderly steel structure lined in glass, Confucian simplicity was combined with Modernist thinking. • The house was in a state of disrepair and the hierarchy of spaces did not work. The new owner was keen to lighten the palette, open up the boxed-in kitchen and create lavish, glossy hotel-style bathrooms. The living areas were rearranged and the service areas were re-worked to fit in with the scale of the house. The kitchen, the hub of the double-height pavilion that serviced the dining room on one side and an informal living room on the other, was redefined as a linear open-ended strip, all white gloss, Calacutta marble and stainless steel. All lighting was concealed to veil the perimeter windows in a soft glowing light at night. • The 3-metre-long dining table was custom-made in highly polished Macassar ebony timber. This richly figured timber was carried through to the back of the house on the timber wall panelling in the study and television room. Centralised in this timber box is the mirrored bathroom, complete with concealed overhead shower and timber deck flooring to match the swimming pool. • The swimming pool and deck area was designed as a luxury 'resort style' pampering area that is tranquil and relaxing. The decking, combined with sawn cut bluestone and modernist Eames fibreglass chairs, provides a great entertaining area, complete with barbeque. • The solid concrete-rendered building at the front of the property was painted Japanese black, giving the building a strong graphic quality. The negative spaces of the black backdrops were used to create contemplation gardens of exquisite lightness. The outdoor incorporation of art that might usually appear inside reinforces the Oriental feeling. • The relentlessly organised design, combined with its modern Asian aesthetic, creates a glamorous and peaceful environment in which to live. The attention to detail is evident throughout and provides a seamless transition from outdoors to indoors.

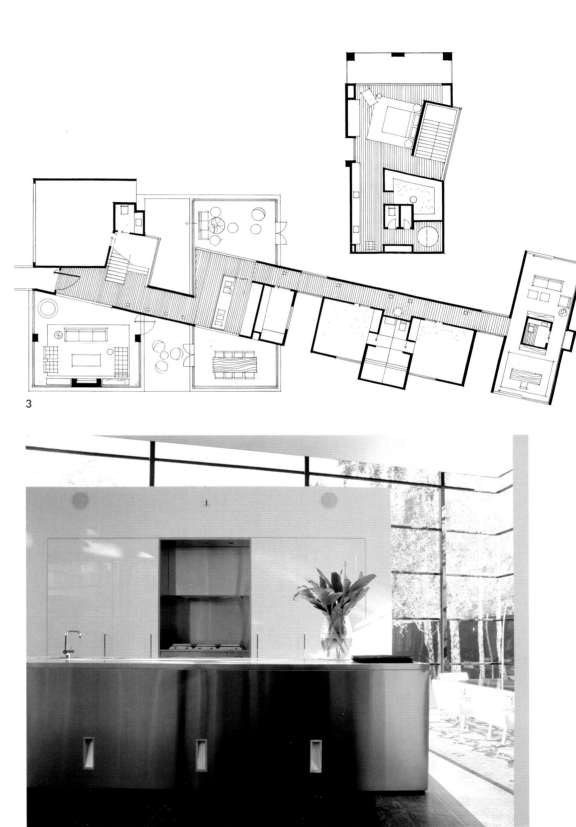

3

4

5

6

7

Photography: Trevor Mein

8

9

10

11

1

1   House nestles into the national park
2   Articulated roof lines create a dynamic yet subtle form on the landscape
3   First floor plan
4   Ground floor plan
5   Lower ground floor plan

TWIST HOUSE

SPACE CUBED ARCHITECTURE STUDIO

Designed for a family of five, the Twist House is sculpted onto an extremely steep hillside site overlooking the **Gold Coast** coastline, and nestles imperceptibly into the forecourt of a national park. The house is an assembly of spaces, dynamically sculpted into forms and masses around a central three-storey circulation node. The design incorporates the architects' belief that the built form should have as little visual and topographic impact on the landscape as possible, as well as addressing climatic conditions and requirements. • The arrangement and articulation of spaces and forms was specifically designed to allow the house to simultaneously shelter and protect for both privacy and climatic reasons and expose and reveal for indoor–outdoor living, climate and views. • The vision was for a combination of raw and standard building materials to convey depth, texture and materiality while emphasising articulation of form and reduction of mass and scale. In bringing these concepts to fruition, the architects proposed a similar technique to meccano set construction: preparing each stage or module of the structural steel framework and then assembling it on site, forming a structural framework within which the residence could materialise, tenuously gripping the steep ridge and overlooking the magnificent views. • This approach also minimised site labour costs and allowed the incorporation of fixing points for scaffolding to avoid the considerable cost of scaffolding from natural ground level some 8 metres below the lowest floor level. The materials too allowed for cost efficiencies either through simple finishing or, in the case of the ply cladding, providing required bracing as well as the finished façade. The curved form of the concrete block wall not only created an architectural expression but also allowed for substantial anchoring of the building below the shale and into natural rock as well as bracing. Its natural finish meant no additional finishing cost or long-term scaffolding.

3

4

5

2

6

7

8

9

6 Consideration for and combination of materials, together with careful detailing, results in rich texture, depth and warmth
7 Feature framing punctuates flowing spaces and characterises individual spaces and uses
8 All spaces are linked by a three-storey stair, bridge and void combination
9 A neutral palette and natural 'warm' materials emphasise connections between spaces
10 Outdoor living areas project towards the views and are elevated above the steep slope
11 Entry space offers glimpses of surrounding views through strategic opening and windows

Photography: John Mills

10

11

1   Kitchen area is integrated to create flush surfaces
2   *Shoji* division between bedroom and hall
3   Front entrance by night featuring the natural elements
4   *Shoji* screen wall, allowing integration between hall and bedrooms

2

1

URUSHI HOUSE

This contemporary house, set amongst the tea-tree on **Victoria's Mornington Peninsula**, merges the elements of a Japanese house with Western style, to create a modern but practical home. • Several key Japanese design elements were implemented in this project, including the use of a *genkan*, a lowered entry level where shoes are removed. Rice paper doors (*shoji*), create a warmth and essence to a room and provide an innovative way of using a hall as part of a bedroom when the screens are set aside. A traditional Japanese sit-down bathroom with low taps and showers, allows one to take a sit-down shower – wooden seats and bowls are provided. • Simplicity and freedom from clutter appear throughout. Timber panelled walls hide doors, cabinetry and stairways. The bedroom floors have a sisal carpet that follows the pattern structure of traditional rice straw Tatami mats. Other natural materials, including timber, stone, water, paper and glass are used extensively. • The openness of Japanese design, where inside and outside often blend and where nature is observed and focused upon, is used throughout. One example is the master bedroom and study, that both look through framed sliding windows with extended walls, focusing concentration on the immediate tea-tree landscape. • The four levels designate the different spaces without overlap of usage. The ground level includes two bedrooms with a shared ensuite. From the entry, a timber step leads to a split level and on to a study. This allows business traffic direct access from the entry without interfering with the household. This second level also incorporates a powder room and laundry. The third level is devoted to spacious open-plan living; the kitchen and dining area form one end of this room and open onto a large deck. Through a kitchen panel, a staircase leads to the master bedroom with a Japanese bathroom to one side and a private tree-top viewing window to the other.

3

4

5

6

7

8

9

10

11

5   The striking façade is a mixture of natural elements
6   Feature fireplace – integrated window
       mullion/mantel/balustrade capping
7   Master cellar by Cellar Creations
8   Hidden entrance to the master retreat through the
       kitchen cabinetry
9   Japanese feature bathroom with sit down showers
10   The wooden panelled wall hides all
11   Ensuite/pond integration – pebble and resin top
       mirrors external pond

**Photography: Mark Munro (1–6,8–10);
Robert Rolls (7,11)**

1

2

3

VAUGHAN RESIDENCE

ROTHELOWMAN

Located on a large block in **Brighton, Victoria**, this property provided an opportunity to experiment with form, space and texture on a large scale and in a diverse suburban context. • The 570-square-metre house is comprised of a number of zones. These zones are, in certain cases, clearly defined, proclaiming their unambiguous use to visitors and occupants alike, while at other times the zones are less rigid, providing for a more fluid transition between less formal areas where usage is high and interaction common. • The internal arrangement of spaces is expressed in the external arrangement of forms with the planning and circulation of the house organised around a central axis. This is defined at the entry by a dominant, double-height, bluestone arch. This axis links the entry with the rear garden and is also used to separate, at ground level, the formal living and entertainment area from the less formal living and dining zone. At first-floor level the axis separates the main bedroom area from the other sleeping and recreational areas. The axis provides a sense of openness, dissolving as it exits the house and moves through a colonnade, eventually terminating at a water feature in the rear garden. • Materially, the intent was to create a contemporary feel with an emphasis on materials with an enduring, low-maintenance quality. Externally, the rendered precast concrete walls were chosen for their economy and suitability for creating the intended architectural forms. Other materials, such as timber, stone and Alucobond panels were chosen for their durability, colour and textural differences. Internally the materials were chosen according to use and location, with the public areas incorporating rich, luxurious and textured materials while the private areas received a modest treatment.

4

1   House from pool area at night
2   View from garden water feature towards rear entry along central axis
3   Front façade from southwest corner of site
4   View of rear façade from garden area
5   Ground floor plan
6   First floor plan

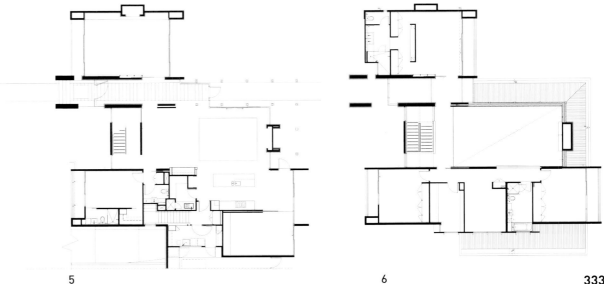

5

6

7

7   Front façade from northwest corner of site
8   Oblique view of rear façade from south site boundary
9   Looking towards informal living and dining area from meals area
10   View across kitchen area towards informal living and dining area

Photography: Aaron Pocock Photography

8

9

10

1

VENN STREET RESIDENCE

HARTREE + ASSOCIATES ARCHITECTS

On a comparatively small lot in an **elite Perth suburb**, the client's intention was to audaciously challenge predictable local constructions, enjoy usage of the entire site, involve the existing palm tree in the experience and provide a clear separation between public and private domains of the home, a delineation defined by the off-form concrete spine wall. • The organisation of internal spaces spills out physically and visually to adjacent outdoor spaces with views to other components of the building, nature and people, helping to extend internal volume. The components of the building harmonise to generate a visual and tactile play of light and an enlivened warmth from within through an interplay of geometric planes, gravity and suspension. • The primary element is anchored in the grassed entry court and dominates the entry sequence. Penetrating and defining an elastic thermal membrane between two distinct volumes, it unfurls to reveal the length of the pool and concludes by plunging into it. There are two distinct modes of living: private/intimate spaces for small groups, and bolder entertaining spaces for larger groups of friends and family. The private spaces are located in an independent structure linked at the entry gallery to the remainder of the home. A two-storey rectilinear element houses formal entertaining spaces, study, vertical circulation and garage, with bedrooms above and is suspended over the garage pavilion to address the street. • An open staircase leads to the private domain, housing the master bedroom, two secondary bedrooms and bathrooms. This component is a linear form running longitudinally against the southern boundary and floating above the entry. The swimming pool was required for exercise (as a lap pool) and as a visual highlight appearing to 'touch the building' and positioned to accentuate the separation of the two building forms.

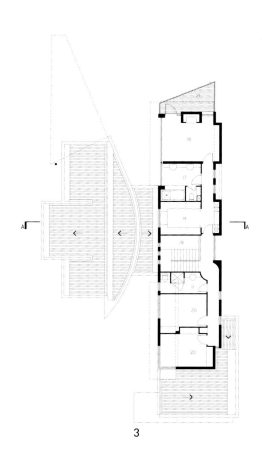

3

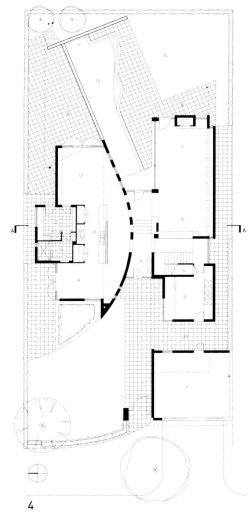

4

1	Entry gate	11	Bathroom
2	Garage	12	Laundry
3	Study	13	Family room
4	Store	14	Lawn
5	Entry/gallery	15	Lap pool
6	Dining	16	Master bedroom
7	Living	17	Ensuite
8	Terrace	18	Walk-in robe
9	Meals	19	Void
10	Kitchen	20	Bedroom
		21	Balcony

1   Lap pool flanked by upper and lower terraces
2   Private landscaped entry space
3   Upper level floor plan
4   Ground level floor plan

2

5 Off-form concrete wall captures winter sun
6 Spine wall defines the entry sequence
7 Internal spaces outlook onto private open space
8 Juxtaposition of forms, materials and finishes
9 Glimpse view to private domains
10 Entry by night
11 Street entry

**Photography: Robert Frith,
Acorn Photo Agency**

5

6

7

8

9

10

11

1

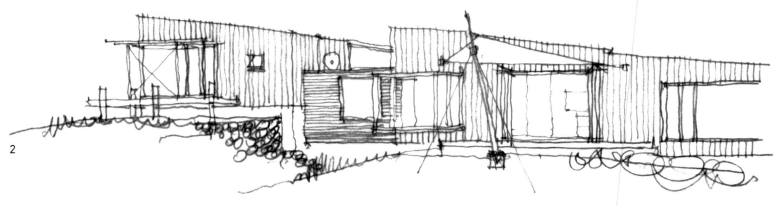

2

3

4

WAIMARIE

IRVING JACK ARCHITECTS

Waimarie ('peaceful waters') sits close to the mouth of a tidal creek near **Nelson** at the top of New Zealand's South Island. The site's subtle beauty encompasses the estuarine creek with its shingle and gentle tidal drift, reeded banks, silvering tide-cast driftwood, remnant flood channels and longer vistas north to the sea and south to the mountains. • The challenge was how to raise the house to capture the longer views without disrupting the character of the landscape. First thoughts were that a sense of partial embedment might suggest the house had arrived through the processes of nature, rather than being deposited there by man. • Waimarie therefore evolved as a 'stranding', as though left after flood. Soil excavated in preparing the long driveway was mounded against the concrete walls of the garage. Anchoring riverstone gabion walls, commonly used for flood control, retain the soil and extend from the upstream end to regulate arrival and entry. The master bedroom and office rise above to command the longer sea and mountain vistas. • Referencing simple utilitarian farm buildings of the surrounding area, the long, low monopitch forms connect easily with the ground. Their orientation was determined by prevailing winds so that the house could effectively create its own shelter. Broad shaded living decks extend out into the landscape on both sides to allow choices of outdoor living depending on weather. • Within, every space is enlivened by openings carefully placed to frame views and to flood the interior with light. Large wrap-around corner bays expand views into the landscape and set up a visual dialogue between adjacent wings. Windows on the long northeast wall capture sun during the day so that in winter, the house is adequately heated by just a wood burner. Both sides of the living areas open up for air movement, and small opening windows combine ventilation with security when the owners are absent.

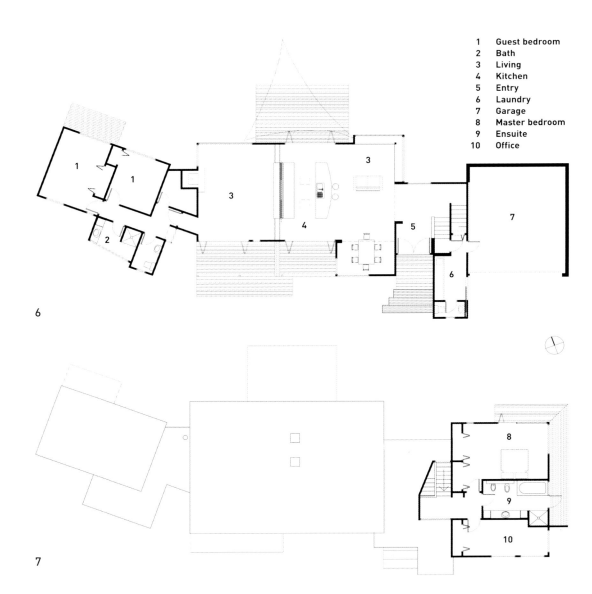

1	Guest bedroom
2	Bath
3	Living
4	Kitchen
5	Entry
6	Laundry
7	Garage
8	Master bedroom
9	Ensuite
10	Office

6

7

5

1   A tensioned sail protects the living deck from afternoon sun
2   Architect's sketch
3   Central kitchen opens to outdoor decks and living spaces
4   Living room floor steps down to provide a sense of intimacy
5   A metal sunscreen provides shade to the master bedroom windows
6   Ground floor plan
7   Upper floor plan

Photography: Elspeth Collier

1

2

3

WAVERLEY RESIDENCE

CULLEN FENG

The existing row of sandstone terraces was built by Ebenezer Vickery in 1866 for the workers in his tannery. Known as 'Glenrock Terrace', it is the oldest surviving terrace in the **Waverley** area and is considered one of the best examples of a stone terrace in **Sydney**. • The existing house had an an unsympathetic rear addition, which was demolished. The front part of the house was unaltered structurally. The brief was to provide a new living area and kitchen, two additional bedrooms, two bathrooms, and a courtyard with rear lane access. Other priorities were to introduce as much natural light as possible, and to distil the original character of the retained part of the house. • The site is a narrow, level, long site with an east–west orientation. A new addition was conceived as a separate pavilion with a modern quality, linked to the original part of the house through an original opening. With Council setback requirements being 900 millimetres in some areas, it was decided that the best spatial solution for all rooms was to have the main stair as a double-flight stair with winders perpendicular to the length of the building, rather than a single-flight stair parallel to the length of the building. This also achieves a fairly generous kitchen. • In the original part of the house, the wall linings were stripped to reveal the original coarse sandstone blocks. The sandstone was given a light clean and then sealed. The original fireplaces were unblocked and revealed; original mouldings were retained. The exposed sandstone adds texture to the house and heightens the contrast between the old and the new. Daylight is introduced via skylights, the stair void and the rear bifolding doors. The new addition has rendered masonry walls, metal deck roofing and aluminium-framed windows and doors. • The front landscaping was treated quite formally, again to respect the historical feel, and to provide a contrast to the rear of the property.

4

1 View of kitchen from living area
2 Kitchen with mirrored splashback
3 Rear view of new two-storey addition at dusk
4 The front original rooms have newly exposed sandstone walls
5 Upper level floor plan
6 Ground level floor plan

Photography: Murray Fredericks

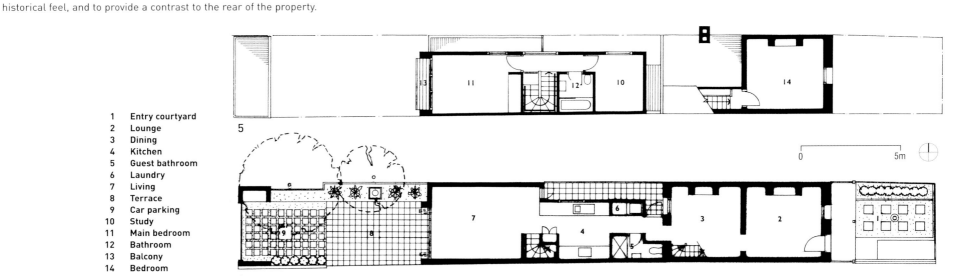

1 Entry courtyard
2 Lounge
3 Dining
4 Kitchen
5 Guest bathroom
6 Laundry
7 Living
8 Terrace
9 Car parking
10 Study
11 Main bedroom
12 Bathroom
13 Balcony
14 Bedroom

5

6

0   5m

1

2

3

4

5

YALLINGUP BEACH HOUSE
CRAIG STEERE ARCHITECTS

The client brief for this beach house at the base of the **Yallingup Beach** hill was to create maximum space and accommodation for at least two families on the restricted site and to take full advantage of the spectacular coastal outlook. • The design and shape of the dwelling was a process of natural evolution, directly reflecting the strict constraints placed by the local municipality. From these formal restrictions the main staggered body and angular roof line followed the angled street boundary. The upper and lower viewing platforms were then twisted and orientated towards the main surf break to the southwest. This created a natural large cantilever in the balcony and roof planes to offer protection from the western sun and winter weather. Recessed outdoor living spaces were then sculptured into the building to offer protection from the prevailing sea breezes. • To enhance protection from the late afternoon sun and sea breeze, automatic external shade fabric roller blinds, controlled by sun and wind sensors, have been fitted to the upper deck, discreetly retracting into concealed recessed troughs within the eaves' lining. • An automatic reticulated window washing system was added to enable 'salt free' clear viewing, and to enhance the durability and life of the aluminium frames. • Simple, durable and practical materials, which offer a subtle but effective aesthetic value, were selected for the interior. They include polished concrete floors, walls finished in the same acrylic render used on external walls, chocolate-coloured Wenge-stained cabinetwork, resin-based terrazzo and limestone tiles. Similarly, durable and maintenance-free materials were selected for the exterior: heavy duty, extra coated Colorbond roofing, flexible coloured textured acrylic brick walls, insitu concrete paving. The materials create a minimal external palette that connects the structure to the coastal vegetation.

6

7

1 View of front elevation from north
2 Kitchen
3 View from southwest
4 View from north
5 Dining and living areas with ocean views
6 Living and dining areas with kitchen beyond
7 Ensuite with ocean views beyond

Photography: Jenny Norton

ARCHITECT CONTACT DETAILS

Andrew Lister Architect   **238**
PO Box 91793, Auckland Mail Centre
Auckland, New Zealand
+64 9 307 7050
andrewlister1@mac.com

Architect Prineas   **314**
Studio 504, 19a Boundary Street
Rushcutters Bay NSW 2011, Australia
+61 2 9332 2006
mail@architectprineas.com.au   www.architectprineas.com.au

Architecture Workshop Ltd   **94**
L3, 78 Victoria Street
Wellington, New Zealand
+64 4 473 4438
email@archwksp.co.nz   www.architectureworkshop.co.nz

Bayden Goddard Design (BGD)   **134, 182**
Suite 65 Commercial Centre
17 Via Roma
Isle of Capri Qld 4217, Australia
+61 7 5592 6188
bgd@bgdarchitects.com   www.bgdarchitects.com

BBP Architects   **310**
7/25 Argyle Street
Fitzroy Vic 3065, Australia
+61 3 9416 1486
info@bbparchitects.com   www.bbparchitects.com

Bevin + Slessor Architects Ltd   **162, 242**
PO Box 33 333, Petone
Wellington, New Zealand
+64 4 568 8669
info@bevinslessor.co.nz   www.bevinslessor.co.nz

Black Kosloff Knott Architects   **268**
Total House, Level 9, 180 Russell Street
Melbourne Vic 3000, Australia
+61 3 9671 4555
office@b-k-k.com.au   www.b-k-k.com.au

Bligh Voller Nield   **66, 144, 148**
365 St Paul's Terrace
Fortitude Valley Qld 4006, Australia
+61 7 3852 2525
shane_thompson@bvn.com.au   www.bvn.com.au

Bourne + Blue Architecture   **204**
PO Box 295
Newcastle NSW 2300, Australia
+61 2 4929 1450
bourneblue@netexcel.net.au

Breathe Architecture   **138**
151 Sydney Road
Brunswick Vic 3056, Australia
+61 3 9381 2007
jeremy@breathe.com.au   www.breathe.com.au

Cassandra Complex   **60**
51 O'Connell Street
North Melbourne Vic 3051, Australia
+61 3 9329 8308
staff@cassandracomplex.com.au   www.cassandracomplex.com.au

CH (Carabott Holt) Architects   **24**
Level 1, 73 Langridge Street
Collingwood Vic 3066, Australia
+ 61 3 9417 1944
info@charchitects.com.au

Connor + Solomon Architects   **32, 40**
Warehouse 5, 37 Nicholson Street
Balmain East NSW 2041, Australia
+61 2 9810 1329
coso@coso.com.au   www.coso.com.au

Corben Architects   **188**
Suite 14, 40 Yeo Street
Neutral Bay NSW 2089, Australia
+61 2 9904 1844
mail@corben.com.au   www.corben.com.au

Cowland North Architecture Interiors Design   **280**
40 Rose Street
Fitzroy Vic 3065, Australia
+61 3 9974 4477
mail@nowarchitecture.com   www.nowarchitecture.com

Coy & Yiontis Pty Ltd   **252**
Level 2/387 Clarendon Street
South Melbourne Vic 3205, Australia
+61 3 9645 7600
cy@cyarchitects.com.au   www.cyarchitects.com.au

Craig Steere Architects   **294, 344**
Suite 9, 219 Onslow Road
Shenton Park WA 6008, Australia
+61 8 9380 4662
craig@craigsteerearchitects.com.au   www.craigsteerearchitects.com.au

Croudace Architects   **64**
Suite 2, 33 Broadway
Nedlands WA 6009, Australia
+61 8 9284 8896
ben@croudacearchitects.com   www.croudacearchitects.com

Cullen Feng Pty Ltd   **248, 298, 342**
104/27 Abercrombie Street
Chippendale NSW 2008, Australia
+61 2 9310 4365
cullenfeng@cullenfeng.com.au   www.cullenfeng.com.au

d.LINEATE architecture + interior design   **166**
PO Box 761
Stirling SA 5152, Australia
+61 8 8339 6644
design@thomsonaustring.com.au

Dale Jones-Evans Pty Ltd Architecture   **106**
Loft 1, 50–54 Ann Street
Surry Hills NSW 2010, Australia
+61 2 9211 0626
dje@dje.com.au   www.dje.com.au

Dalman Architecture   **90**
329 Durham Street
Christchurch, New Zealand
+64 3 366 5445
rd@dalman.co.nz   www.dalman.co.nz

David Hicks Pty Ltd   **20, 22, 320**
PO Box 6110, Chapel Street North
South Yarra Vic 3141, Australia
+61 3 9826 3955
david@davidhicks.com.au   www.davidhicks.com.au

Dawson Brown Architecture   **54, 158**
Level 1, 63 William Street
East Sydney NSW 2010, Australia
+61 2 9360 7977
dba@dawsonbrownarchitecture.com   www.dawsonbrownarchitecture.com

DEM (Aust) Pty Ltd   **178**
115 Sailors Bay Road
Northbridge NSW 2063, Australia
+61 2 8966 6000
sydney@dem.com.au   www.dem.com.au

DesignInc Perth Pty Ltd   **114**
PO Box 924
West Perth WA 6872, Australia
+61 8 9322 3199
ccj@perth.designinc.com.au   www.designinc.com.au

Design King Company Pty Ltd   **284**
Unit 102, 21 Alberta Street
Sydney NSW 2000, Australia
+61 2 9261 3062
jonking@netspace.net.au   www.designking.com.au